Developing Critical Cultural Competence

We would like to dedicate this book to all the students, teachers, and families we have worked with over the years from whom we have learned so much and without whom this book would not be possible. We would also like to thank our own families who continue to support us in doing this work, and acknowledge the contributions of our many colleagues who share our vision for a more equitable environment in our schools.

Developing Critical Cultural Competence

A Guide for 21st-Century Educators

Jewell E. Cooper
Ye He
Barbara B. Levin

Foreword by
Christine Sleeter

**Includes Online
Facilitator Toolkit**

CORWIN
A SAGE Company

CORWIN
A SAGE Company

FOR INFORMATION:

Corwin
A SAGE Company
2455 Teller Road
Thousand Oaks, California 91320
(800) 233-9936
Fax: (800) 417-2466
www.corwin.com

SAGE Ltd.
1 Oliver's Yard
55 City Road
London EC1Y 1SP
United Kingdom

SAGE India Pvt. Ltd.
B 1/I 1 Mohan Cooperative
Industrial Area
Mathura Road, New Delhi 110 044
India

SAGE Asia-Pacific Pte. Ltd.
33 Pekin Street #02-01
Far East Square
Singapore 048763

Acquisitions Editor: Debra Stollenwerk
Associate Editor: Desirée A. Bartlett
Editorial Assistant: Kimberly Greenberg
Project Editor: Veronica Stapleton
Copy Editor: Codi Bowman
Typesetter: C&M Digitals (P) Ltd.
Proofreader: Wendy Jo Dymond
Indexer: Jean Casalegno
Cover Designer: Rose Storey
Permissions Editor: Adele Hutchinson

Printed in the United States of America.

Library of Congress Cataloging-in-Publication Data

Cooper, Jewell E.

Developing critical cultural competence : a guide for 21st-century educators / Jewell E. Cooper, Ye He, Barbara B. Levin ; foreword by Christine Sleeter.

p. cm.
Summary: "This book shows you how to provide professional development for teachers that deepens their cultural understanding and includes activities for translating new knowledge into action. Companion website available"— Provided by publisher.

Includes bibliographical references and index.

ISBN 978-1-4129-9625-9 (pbk.)

1. Multicultural education—United States. 2. Cultural competence—United States. 3. Teachers—Training of—United States. I. He, Ye, Dr. II. Levin, Barbara B. III. Title.

LC1099.3.C665 2011 370.1170973—dc23 2011025626

This book is printed on acid-free paper.

11 12 13 14 15 10 9 8 7 6 5 4 3 2 1

Contents

Additional resources related to *Developing Critical Cultural Competence* can be found at www.corwin.com/culturalcompetence

List of Resources

The following Resources can be accessed at the companion website for *Developing Critical Cultural Competence: A Guide for 21st-Century Educators*, www.corwin.com/culturalcompetence.

Foreword

Christine Sleeter

California State University Monterey Bay

Teachers were filing into the cafeteria as my colleague and I were setting up the projector. We had been invited to this racially diverse middle school to help the predominantly White teaching staff confront the "grades gap" (the gap in report card letter grades between White students and students of color, which had been the subject of a newspaper exposé) and to analyze why students of color, on average, not only received lower grades than White students but were also being overreferred for disciplinary action and special education. My colleague and I arrived armed with data for both the school and the school district levels. Our plan was to present the data, invite teachers to consider why there was a racial gap in student outcomes in their school, and then consider strategies to address the gap.

Within 10 minutes, however, it became apparent that this workshop was not going to go well. While the few Black teachers, along with a handful of White teachers, nodded their heads affirmatively as we talked, several White male teachers sitting near the back of the room, arms folded, glared at us. After we briefly presented the data and then invited discussion, only a few teachers spoke. While some comments focused on what the school could do differently, most characterized the Black students as poorly behaved and their parents as lacking much interest in education. Although my colleague and I expected to hear some deficit thinking from teachers, given that we had been invited to do this workshop, we were unprepared for the wall of hostile silence most of the teachers maintained and the rapidity with which discussion turned into defensive complaints.

How I wish that *Developing Critical Cultural Competence* by Cooper, He, and Levin had been available at that time! This story, which is true, repeats itself countless times, with minor variations. Not only have I found myself doing less-than-helpful professional development workshops, over the years, I have also read about and talked with many colleagues who have done the same. Although research on professional development for multicultural education confirms that short-term workshops, like the one discussed previously, are virtually useless and even counterproductive (McDiarmid, 1992), they continue to occur. This is probably largely because while many school leaders recognize diversity and equity problems within their schools and hear about "experts" who seem have solutions, lacking a strategy to engage teachers with core issues around difference and equity, school leaders hope that bringing in an expert will help. Too often missing, however, is a well-conceptualized approach for professional development for cross-cultural competence.

Research on professional development for multicultural education gives some clues about what does and does not make a positive difference. Professional development projects that are too broad, attempting to rework teachers' worldviews about issues such as race and justice, are often met with resistance and conflict, even if they are ongoing rather than single workshops (Leistyna, 2001; Sleeter, 1992). Inquiry-based professional development that includes critical reflection is much more likely to make an impact on teachers (El-Haj, 2003; Estrada, 2005; Jennings & Smith, 2002; Moss, 2001; Nieto, 2003; Sleeter, 2009). Community-based learning, which is quite underused, can be a powerful form of professional development (Fickel, 2005; Moll & González, 1994).

What would such professional development look like, especially if it is designed to prompt teachers to grapple with something as emotionally charged as race, racism, and gaps in student outcomes and school experiences? What might it look like if the professional development also addresses a range of forms of diversity including religion, gender equity, sexual orientation, and social class?

Developing Critical Cultural Competence shows what this kind of professional development looks like, and it provides the tools to make it happen. In this marvelous book, Cooper, He, and Levin lay out a system that begins with teachers unpacking diversity in their lives, and then moving outward to consider their students, their school, and the communities the school serves. The activities in this book, which the authors have used often and refined, are very well conceptualized to engage teachers in learning, thinking, and reflecting about what can be highly emotional and threatening issues. By offering choices and scaffolding sense-making, the activities treat teachers as adults who are capable of learning and looking at problems from different points of view. By offering structured ways to learn from students and communities, the activities help teachers develop their learning strategies, as well as strategies that have the potential to build bridges of ongoing communication among teachers, students, and communities.

Although this book is written for professional developers, I see it as having a wide audience. For school leaders who see problems related to equity and diversity but aren't sure what to do about them, this book will show a very helpful professional development process. Preservice teacher educators will find many useful resources between these covers; as a preservice teacher educator myself, I have used strategies similar to many of these and have identified others in this book I will relish trying. This book can also be useful to teachers who may not be part of an organized professional development program but who want to understand their students better and are looking for guidance.

These days, especially, when much teacher professional development (at least, where I live) involves showing teachers how to use curriculum packages and testing systems, *Developing Critical Cultural Competence* offers a refreshing alternative and an inspiring view of teaching, teachers, students, and the process of learning.

Preface

Why do we need this book?

With an increasingly diverse population of students in today's schools, and the fact that most teachers remain predominantly White, female, monolingual, and middle class, it is imperative that all educators move beyond simple, declarative knowledge about our students' family and community backgrounds toward a deeper, more critical understanding of the complexities that affect their lives. In fact, this is true no matter who the children are that you are in the business of educating. To improve academic achievement for all students, it is vital that educators develop a more nuanced understanding of themselves as cultural beings and the habit of critical reflection regarding ways of knowing about themselves, their students, their families, and the communities they serve. Looking at data is not enough. We have to know who our students are! Therefore, 21st-century educators need to develop critical cultural competence, a beyond-knowledge understanding based on critical reflection of self, students, families, and communities. With critical cultural competence as a base, educators can finally take appropriate actions to lead the change needed to provide more accessible and equitable learning environments for all students, which ultimately are what is needed to improve academic achievement. We believe this can be accomplished best through ongoing professional development for both new and experienced teachers and administrators, no matter the context in which they teach, which is why we wrote this book for professional developers.

Furthermore, the Obama administration's proposed blueprint for reauthorizing the Elementary and Secondary Education Act (ESEA) makes this book timely because it reenvisions education with a strong focus on (1) meeting the needs of diverse learners and (2) supporting comprehensive approaches to family engagement, and it includes

(3) funding professional development relevant to these topics. In addition to promoting "specific programs designed to involve families and communities and through policies that will empower and engage families," the Obama administration's proposal "encourages professional development programs to improve teachers' and leaders' skills in working with families" (Department of Education, 2010, p. 3). With this in mind, this book provides professional development personnel with numerous strategies that will strengthen teacher–school–family partnerships to increase student success.

What is critical cultural competence?

Critical cultural competence means going well beyond awareness or just knowing *about* the diversity of students in today's schools. It means developing a deep, nuanced, and complex understanding of diversity and becoming skilled in cross-cultural communication by (1) engaging in private and public opportunities for self-reflection to surface implicit personal biases and assumptions and understanding why they exist; (2) negotiating understanding within and across cultural groups to promote learning; and (3) transforming local educational settings through thoughtful, innovative practices that enhance equity to ensure engagement and achievement. While culturally competent educators reflect on their practices and seek knowledge about their students, families, and communities, educators with critical cultural competence are more considered in their reflections, more innovative in taking action that is meaningful and directly related to motivating and engaging their students, and more collaborative in reforming and transforming their schools' culture to meet the needs of *all* learners. Further, we believe the ultimate goal of developing critical cultural competence is transforming local educational settings through thoughtful, innovative, and responsive practices that enhance equity in education for all.

We realize that only by taking a lead role in school and district reform initiatives will educators really achieve critical cultural competence. We also know that many educators are not yet ready to make the kinds of changes needed to educate today's diverse population of students. However, we believe that by wholeheartedly engaging in sustained professional development, as described in this book, they can become educators who are able to meet the needs of today's and tomorrow's diverse learners. Therefore, we offer activities to build a bridge from typical multicultural education provided in the past to more critical cultural competence needed today. Instead of only offering educators *what* they need to know about cultural diversity, we go beyond knowledge to highlight *how* educators can identify their beliefs, goals, and visions to acquire usable knowledge about their students' backgrounds and to see their students' families and communities as valuable resources for helping educate them. We hope this book will be the first step in actually facilitating educators to develop critical cultural competence, and we offer many tried-and-tested, in-depth activities toward this end that other books do not. Several of these activities require educators to move physically from their classrooms and schools into their students' home communities so they can learn firsthand about the strengths of the environment in which their students' reside and in which their first education about the world occurs. For some, this will feel daunting, but we have learned that it is a necessary part of building critical cultural competence.

Who is this book for?

The audience for this book is primarily professional development staff, including lead teachers, district- and building-level administrators, and emerging teacher leaders who believe more thought and action is needed and who want to engage teachers and administrators in developing their critical cultural competence. Teacher educators looking for activities to push both preservice and inservice teachers' critical reflections about themselves, their students, and the families and communities of their students are another audience for this book.

How is this book different from other books about diversity and multicultural education?

Most books about multicultural education and cross-cultural competence describe *what* educators need to know about a multitude of cultural groups. This book goes beyond knowledge and well beyond addressing multiculturalism in our schools using a limited "heroes and holidays" curriculum to present ways to develop critical cultural competence. We have compiled a multitude of activities that go beyond what is typically offered in most books about multicultural education, making it a useful guide for planning and leading professional development around issues of diversity and critical cultural competence to help today's students achieve their potential.

Organization and Special Features of This Book

The approach we take is to provide detailed examples of numerous activities we have used over the years in the three areas we focus on in our work: (1) understanding the self (Chapters 2 and 3), (2) understanding our students (Chapters 4 and 5), and (3) learning from families and the community (Chapters 6 and 7). Chapters 2, 4, and 6 include activities that enhance educators' awareness and understanding *about* themselves, their students, and the families and communities of their students. In Chapters 3, 5, and 7, we offer additional activities that will extend educators' experiences and critical thinking with the goal of moving them beyond their comfort level by engaging in more critical and transformative thoughts and actions regarding diversity issues. Chapter 1 describes five key concepts recently proposed by Milner (2010) as foundational to the curriculum for all diversity courses or workshops, and revisits many typical approaches for professional development about multicultural education and diversity issues. Chapter 8 includes a discussion of critical cultural competence and its relationship to culturally responsive teaching, and it provides several sample professional development plans to demonstrate how the activities in this book can be used in systematic efforts toward the transformation of school cultures. Measures and indicators for success are also shared for ongoing evaluation of the effectiveness of sustained professional development efforts.

In Chapters 1 through 7, we include the objective(s) for each activity, instructions for participants, recommended discussion questions for both individual reflection and group discussion, approximate time allotments for completing each activity, and tips for those facilitating the activity based on our personal experiences. In the companion website for this book, www.corwin.com/culturalcompetence, we also provide reproducible resource lists and handouts to support many activities, as well as examples that can serve as models for some of the activities. Throughout the book, you will find web resource icons indicating that a related resource can be found on the website. Additionally, at the end of each chapter, you will find a list of web resources corresponding to that chapter.

An extensive reference list and an additional list of the authors' favorite resources are also included for professional development leaders who want to go more in-depth. Based on our experiences with the challenges and the impact of preparing teachers to be more critically culturally competent, we also include the voices of teachers who have experienced many of these activities and/or our experience with handling potential issues that facilitators may encounter when using some of the more challenging activities.

Other special features in this book include questions for reflection and extension by those facilitating professional development geared toward building critical cultural competence in themselves and others, suggestions for how activities can be used most effectively in Professional Learning Communities (PLCs), and ideas for modifying some of the activities for use in online professional development.

Conclusion

The main reasons why this book will help those engaged in professional development around building critical cultural competence include the following:

- Professional development is one of the major strategies needed to enhance teachers and administrators' cultural competence if we want them to make the personal connections needed to make their data-driven instructional efforts meaningful and worthwhile.
- Different from isolated or short-term sessions about diversity issues, in-depth and long-term district or school-based professional development provides the best opportunity for teachers and administrators to "to continually reassess what schooling means in the context of a pluralist society; the relationships between teachers and learners; and attitudes and beliefs about language, culture, and race" (Clair & Adger, 1999, p. 2) within authentic teaching contexts.
- Most important, what is learned, shared, and discussed in professional development sessions can have immediate application to curriculum design; material selection; instructional planning; and both teachers' and administrators' daily interactions with peers, diverse students, and their families and communities.
- Finally, professional development efforts to enhance educators' critical cultural competence have the potential to lead to the transformation of school culture and instructional practices that impact both family and community engagement and, ultimately, student achievement.

Acknowledgments

C orwin would like to thank the following individuals for taking the time to provide their editorial insight:

Denise Carlson, Curriculum Consultant
Heartland Area Education Agency
Johnston, IA

Carol Gallegos, Literacy Coach
Hanford Elementary School District
Hanford, CA

Lori Grossman, Academic Trainer/Mentor Program Coordinator
Houston Independent School District
HR/Professional Development Services

Judson Laughter, Assistant Professor of English Education
Department of Theory and Practice in Teacher Education
University of Tennessee
Knoxville, TN

Bess Scott, Director of Elementary Education
Lincoln Public Schools
Lincoln, NE

About the Authors

Dr. Jewell E. Cooper is an Associate Professor in the Teacher Education and Higher Education Department at The University of North Carolina at Greensboro (UNCG) where she also serves as the Coordinator of Secondary Teacher Education. She holds a master's degree in curriculum and instruction from the University of Memphis and a Ph.D. in curriculum and teaching from UNCG. Prior to becoming a faculty member at UNCG, she was an Assistant Professor at Bennett College for Women. A middle school language arts teacher, Dr. Cooper also has public school teaching experience in North Carolina, Michigan, and Tennessee.

Dr. Cooper's research areas include multicultural education, particularly community-based learning and culturally responsive teaching, secondary school reform, and teacher development. She has published several journal articles in national and international journals as well as book chapters in such publications as *Leadership and Building Professional Communities*; *Home, School, and Community Collaboration: Culturally Responsible Family Involvement; and Race, Ethnicity, and Education* (vol. 3).

Dr. Cooper has taught college and university courses in multicultural education, models of teaching and educational psychology. For the past decade, her students have participated in community-based learning. She has conducted professional development related to diverse learners, culturally responsive teaching, inclusive practices, and self-regulated learning for both public and private schools. In 2003, she was awarded the Teaching Excellence Award by the UNCG School of Education, and in 2004, she was awarded the Alumni Teaching Excellence Award by the university.

Dr. Ye He is an Assistant Professor in the Teacher Education and Higher Education Department at the University of North Carolina at Greensboro (UNCG). She holds a PhD in curriculum and instruction with a concentration in teacher education. Before coming to UNCG, she taught English language courses and translation courses in public schools, colleges, and universities in China.

Dr. He currently serves as the English as a Second Language (ESL) teacher education program coordinator at UNCG and teaches linguistics, ESL methods, and cross-cultural communication courses at the graduate level. As one of the co-PIs on a 5-year, $1.4 million National Professional Development grant, she has been engaged in professional development activities with both faculty at the university level and teachers in K–12 settings. In the last three years, she has delivered over 150 hours of professional development sessions on topics including second language development theories and teaching methods, building cultural backgrounds in lesson preparation and delivery, and other linguistic and cultural diversity issues in teaching and learning.

Dr. He's research areas include ESL teacher education, diversity and equity in education, teacher beliefs and development, and the application of strength-based theories in teacher preparation. She has published one book and a number of peer-refereed articles on these topics. Her most recent publications include "Collaboration in Professional Development for ELL Content Achievement" in *AccELLerate* and "Moving Beyond 'Just Good Teaching': ESL Professional Development for All Teachers" published in *Professional Development in Education*.

Dr. Barbara B. Levin began her career in higher education in the Department of Curriculum and Instruction (CUI) at the University of North Carolina at Greensboro (UNCG) in 1993. Prior to attending UC–Berkeley and earning a PhD in Educational Psychology she was an elementary school teacher for 17 years. Her master's degree in curriculum and instruction is from the University of Wisconsin–Madison.

Dr. Levin's research focuses on teacher education, especially understanding how teacher beliefs and teachers' pedagogical understandings develop across their careers. Other research interests include case-based pedagogy, problem–based learning, and teaching and learning with technology. Dr. Levin has published numerous articles in well-respected journals and has also published four books, including a best-selling book with Corwin titled *Leading 21st Century Schools: Harnessing Technology for Engagement and Achievement*.

In addition to her teaching and research, Dr. Levin developed and led online professional development with National Board Certified Teachers (NBCTs) around completing teacher action research projects, and has worked with inservice teachers to focus on unit planning using Backward Design (Wiggins & McTighe, 2005) as part of a 5-year, $1.4 million National Professional Development grant called TESOL for ALL , awarded in 2007 by the U.S. Department of Education.

Dr. Levin was her department's Director of Graduate Studies for eight years, and continues to serve as assistant chair for the Department of Teacher Education and Higher Education (formerly CUI). She is completing her eighth year as associate editor for *Teacher Education Quarterly*, and was awarded the first Mentoring-Advising-Supervising (MAS) Award by the School of Education at UNCG in 2008 for her mentoring of students and faculty members.

Introduction

What Do We Need to Do to Prepare Teachers for Today's Diverse Classrooms?

Given increasing student diversity and gaps in student achievement, we all have to ask, What can we do to enhance the achievement of all students? What should be the focus of professional development to best prepare educators to work effectively with today's diverse student populations? What are some concrete strategies and activities we could adapt and employ in our grade level, at our schools, or in districtwide workshops to truly engage and affect today's educators? Because research indicates that culturally competent educators can improve the success of diverse students at schools (Gay, 2010; C. Grant, Elsbree, & Fondrie, 2004; Ladson-Billings, 1995), it is our intention to offer concrete, interactive, and challenging activities throughout this book to prepare educators, including all kinds of teachers (preservice and inservice) and administrators, to develop their critical cultural competence.

Why do we need educators with critical cultural competence in today's schools?

Growing ethnic, cultural, and linguistic diversity is what describes today's classroom. Furthermore, educators are seeing student diversity that includes much more than ethnic and linguistic differences because of the changing demographics listed here:

- In 2005, immigrants represented one in nine of all U.S. residents, but their children represented one in five of all children younger than age 18 (Capps, Fix, Murray, Ost, Passel, & Herwantoro-Hernandez, 2005).
- In 2009, approximately 17 million school-age children spoke a language other than English at home, and more than 3 million reported problems in speaking English (Rong & Preissle, 2009).
- About 11.3% of the U.S. population was living in poverty in 2005; but 17.6% of children younger than 18 years old lived in poverty (U.S. Census Bureau, 2005).
- Among students and families who were impacted the most by the current economic downturn, women and those from ethnic minority groups or lower socioeconomic classes were disproportionately overrepresented (Shim & Serido, 2010).

In addition to increasing diversity among our student population, educators continue to face pressures from all levels to do more to raise achievement and close the achievement gap that still exists. For example, although the overall reading scores of students based on the National Assessment of Educational Progress (NAEP) data were slightly higher in 2007 than in 1992 and the achievement gaps in reading and mathematics were narrower, White students still had higher scores than Black students (Vanneman, Hamilton, Anderson, & Rahman, 2009). Similarly, even though far more efforts have been devoted to instruction for English Learners (ELs) since No Child Left Behind (NCLB), the academic achievement gap between ELs and their native-English-speaking peers is still significant nationwide.

Given these demographic imperatives, we describe our goals for writing this book by sharing our experiences, strategies, and activities with others interested in developing educators with critical cultural competent.

How can we move professional development *about* diversity beyond knowledge?

With the increasing complexity of student diversity, knowledge about the different facets of diversity is not enough for teachers and administrators to implement meaningful strategies in their daily work with diverse students. Furthermore, all elements of culture intersect with one another to create an environment where individuals' multifaceted identities emerge. As a result, student diversity is becoming increasingly complex. Considering this complexity, it almost becomes more misleading than informative to learn only about characteristics of specific cultural groups because within-group diversity is at least as vast as cross-group differences, if not more.

Take ELs as an example. Students are typically labeled as English as a second language (ESL) or limited English proficiency (LEP) at school because their parents indicated on a form that a different home language is used and the student's English proficiency does not test at the native-speaker level based on the placement test. However, the labels ESL or LEP do not reflect the student's cultural background, reasons for coming to the United States, prior schooling experiences, first-language literacy level, academic content mastery, family socioeconomic level, parents' educational backgrounds, and the like. For example, the needs of a new student born in a refugee camp without formal schooling are very different from sojourner students who visit the United States because of their parents' temporary job assignment, even though both of them may appear to have African, Arabic, or Asian ancestry, are labeled as ESL, and do not seem to participate in classroom discussions.

Even with increasing educators' understanding of the complexity of our students' backgrounds, it is impossible for them to be prepared with exhaustive knowledge about specific combinations of various facets of their students' culture, language, ethnicity, and the like that may be visible, invisible, seen, unseen, recognized, or unrecognized. In professional development, therefore, our goal is not to provide a complete set of facts or list of concepts about diverse learners. Rather, in this book, we aim to develop teachers' competence regarding diversity that goes beyond knowledge. That is, we aim to develop teachers' *critical cultural competence* by enhancing their skills and strategies to evaluate and extend their understandings and practices through reflections and daily interactions with diverse students and families both inside and outside the school building.

Going beyond knowledge of the educator-self, of one's students, and their families and home communities through the professional development activities, we would like to challenge teachers to develop *critical cultural competence*, which entails teachers' abilities to

- engage in self-reflection about their cultural identities and experiences and also in critical reflection to surface personal biases and to form visions and beliefs that guide, and even transform, educational practices in diverse settings;

- explore the cultural backgrounds of their students, families, and the communities and find ways to negotiate their roles as teachers and administrators to leverage students' strengths and assets to maximize learning; and
- transform their individual practices in classrooms, schools, and in other their local educational settings by using systematic, thoughtful, and innovative practices and collaborations.

Who are we in this thing called diversity?

As many researchers have pointed out, educators' reflection is an inseparable part of their professional development. Therefore, before we can talk about what student diversity is and how we could effectively work with diverse students and their families, it is important to first examine the individual, personal lens through which we view today's diverse world and where we see ourselves fitting into the changing sociocultural contexts.

Educators' values and assumptions about student diversity are strongly influenced by their personal experiences within and beyond classrooms settings. Although the majority of today's public school teachers are still White, middle-class females (Zumwalt & Craig, 2005), many have had experiences interacting with people from ethnic, cultural, and linguistic backgrounds different from their own as a result of the changing demographics in the country, globalization, and enhanced use of technology. The widespread use of websites, blogs, wikis, and other forums have broadened our perspectives and made global issues local because of much faster exchanges of information. In addition, educators today also have more opportunities to participate in international exchange programs, to be engaged in intercultural relationships, and to devote time and effort to service in progressively diverse local communities, all of which foster their enhanced appreciation for diversity (Dee & Henkin, 2002; R. W. Smith, 2000). In professional development, it is critical that we build on these new opportunities and experiences that teachers have and be more purposeful in guiding all educators' critical examination of their typically individualistic and meritocratic beliefs. By doing so, teachers and administrators may be able to connect their experiences with diversity to make a shift in their ideologies to reach a deeper understanding of critical cultural competence and to take action for social change.

Through professional development activities that engage educators in critical examination of their beliefs and identities with the goal of increasing self-understanding, they are encouraged not only to be aware of their assumptions and potential biases but also to make explicit their visions, goals, and practical theories that guide their actions and interactions with all students. Therefore, beginning with understanding oneself as a cultural being and developing habits of self-reflection are promoted throughout this book.

How do we leverage assets of students, families, and communities?

In addition to promoting critical self-reflection, we also promote the development of asset-based thinking about diverse students, families, and communities through additional professional development activities that lead to learning about and making use of students' strengths in educating them. Different from merely being positive, asset-based thinking is "based on direct, systematic observation into how a growing minority of highly effective, satisfied people thinks, feels and acts. . . . [It] calls for positive action and traction in the present moment" (Cramer & Wasiak, 2006, p. 15). Applied to professional development and classroom instruction, asset-based instruction highlights students' strengths and requires teachers to focus on both the cognitive and affective development of their students. For example, in Boston public schools, district-level professional development and coaching were provided for secondary mathematics teachers to build on students' strengths and assets (Paek, 2008). Teachers then applied asset-based thinking during their instruction to (1) identify students' mathematics strengths through students' sharing of their previous experiences with mathematics concepts, (2) link new mathematics concepts and procedures explicitly to identified student strengths through teacher demonstrations, and (3) encourage students' reflection on the metacognitive process of learning. This asset-based, strength-based approach not only enhanced students' mathematics achievement but also allowed teachers to truly co-construct positive learning experiences with their students.

In this book, we share professional development activities we have used to develop asset- and strength-based thinking, and include statements from teachers about how these activities have impacted their interactions with students and their families and communities. We believe that the only way to effectively prepare educators with critical cultural competence for all students is to intentionally provide experiences with guided reflections for teachers and administrators to explore ways to become learners of their students and the families within and beyond classroom settings (Delpit, 1995; Gay, 2010).

Bringing It All Together

While other researchers have presented different models for developing teachers' understanding, awareness of, and competence with diversity (J. A. Banks, 2006; Grant & Sleeter, 2006; Jenks, Lee, & Kanpol, 2001; McLaren, 2006; Nieto, 2000), they all emphasize the importance of all educators (1) engaging in critical self-reflection about their assumptions and cultural beliefs, (2) developing deeper understanding of student diversity and assets, and (3) building on the "funds of knowledge" generated through the diverse cultural perspectives and heritage in the communities.

As is shown in Figure FM.1, the goal of developing or enhancing educators' critical cultural competence is to impact instructional practices and to promote the achievement of students, especially those who are culturally, ethnically, and linguistically diverse. Toward this end, the focus of this book is on professional development activities and ideas that facilitate the development of critical cultural competence from the viewpoint of three additional and inseparable aspects: *self*, *students*, and *families and communities*.

These three aspects—self, students, and families and communities— are intertwined through asset-based thinking and innovative collaboration with peers, students, families, and communities to promote teachers' and administrators' ongoing development toward critical cultural competence. In this book, we devote specific chapters for each of the three aspects related to critical cultural competence. Through the professional development activities described in this book, we encourage educators to apply their new understandings and to transform their current instructional practices to promote equity education and, ultimately, enhance the academic success of all students. Figure FM.1 captures the major components that we believe are needed beyond knowledge to promote students' achievement in today's diverse schools.

Figure FM.1 Teacher Critical Cultural Competence

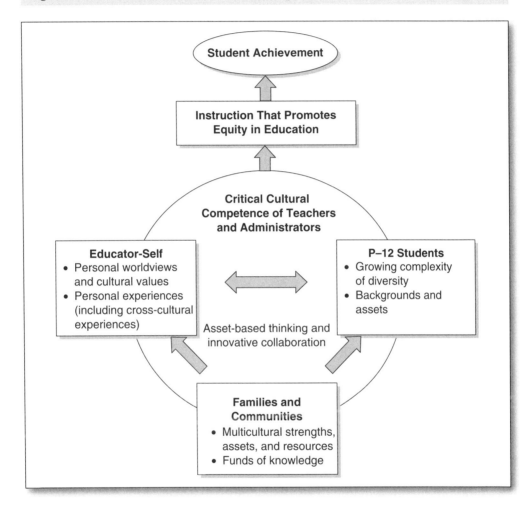

SUMMARY OF KEY POINTS

This introduction includes an overview of the need to help educators develop critical cultural competence in today's increasingly diversity classrooms. The purposes and the theoretical foundations that guide the design of the book are also shared:

- Student diversity is a complex concept, and professional development regarding diversity issues needs to include more than just knowledge about diversity.

- We argue for the importance of developing educators' *critical cultural competence*, which includes the ability to engage in critical reflection of self from alternative perspectives to surface implicit personal biases and assumptions; negotiate understanding within and across cultural groups to promote learning; and transform local educational settings through thoughtful, innovative practices to enhance equity in education.

REFLECTION AND EXTENSION

- Thinking about the teachers and administrators you are working with, what do you think are the major goals and objectives for the professional development on diversity issues?
- What would you like to see because of professional development efforts at your school or in your district?

1

Common Practices

How Are We Currently Preparing Educators for Diverse Classrooms?

Introduction

In this chapter, we discuss several tried-and-true methods for preparing educators to be culturally competent to teach diverse learners in today's multicultural, multilinguistic classrooms by using a variety of readings, videos, discussion topics, and activities designed to help educators become more knowledgeable about the diversity of their students and to build their capacity as culturally responsive educators. To begin, we review several goals commonly used for multicultural education and then describe five key concepts proposed by Milner (2010) for all diversity courses or workshops. We talk about Milner's ideas early because they are key ideas related to our goal of helping educators become *critically* culturally competent. We then review several resources we have used to start educators on their path toward cultural competence. Although the goal of this book is to move multicultural education and diversity training beyond decontextualized knowledge into a more critical exploration of the self, students, their families, and communities, we begin with a discussion of established practices in multicultural education before helping educators begin to develop a deeper and more nuanced understanding of students that includes ways to learn from and value their families and their communities.

Common Goals for Multicultural Education

In recent years, diversity workshops and multicultural education courses typically have some or all of the following goals so that educators will be able to complete the following:

- Demonstrate an awareness of competencies related to educating students from culturally diverse backgrounds based on ethnicity (race, language, national origin, and religion), socioeconomic class, gender, age, and the like
- Analyze the "isms" (e.g., racism, sexism, classism, heterosexism, linguicism, ethnocentrism, ageism, and ableism) and their effect on the practice and the institutionalization of schooling
- Describe the legal, historic, and philosophical basis for educating culturally diverse students
- Assess through analysis of readings, videos, case studies, class discussions, and the like educators' dispositions related to teaching diverse learners and working with their families
- Identify several teaching and learning strategies to accommodate the needs of culturally diverse students
- Analyze and evaluate various culturally responsive teaching practices and environments
- Identify national, state, and local resources available to assist educators in planning and implementing instruction for culturally diverse students

These goals are found in many courses and workshops about diverse learners, but they are not exhaustive or inclusive of everything required to meet the needs of today's diverse population of P–12 learners. In fact, we would include these additional goals to assist educators developing critical cultural competence: (1) critical self-reflection and identity work; (2) engaging wholeheartedly with students, families, and communities to assure equity, achievement, and success for all learners; and (3) engaging in transformative actions that will lead to change in local educational settings.

Foundational Understandings About Diversity

Milner's Five Conceptual Repertoires of Diversity

In this book, we share our ideas for engaging educators in activities that promote the knowledge, skills, and dispositions needed to develop critical cultural competence. Before doing that, however, we introduce key conceptual repertoires needed for developing critical cultural competence. Milner (2010) suggests that the following five concepts should be directly addressed in the curriculum of every diversity course or workshop for educators: (1) *color blindness,* (2) *cultural conflict,* (3) *the myth of meritocracy,* (4) *deficit conceptions,* and (5) *expectations.* Although Milner does not claim this to be an exhaustive list, he suggests that developing a deep and complex understanding of these five "conceptual repertoires" should be the common core for any diversity curriculum (Milner, 2010, p. 119), and we agree wholeheartedly.

Color-blindness. When we hear teachers say, "I don't see color. I just teach children!" we get very concerned because such thinking denies a very important aspect of the identity of children of color; ignores their families' heritage and history; and discounts their larger racial, ethnic, or language community. When some educators say things such as, "I don't see color. I treat all my students the same," they may not realize that the underlying meaning could be the following:

- "I don't see *my* color. I don't want to think about how my racial and ethnic identity may have given me privilege in society."
- "I choose not to see my students' color. I don't want to admit that I may have biases or personal assumptions about certain groups of people. Ignoring my students' racial and ethnic differences allows me not to have to face my biases."
- "I don't feel comfortable talking about racial and ethnic differences because that makes me sound like a racist. My parents taught me not to mention race or racial differences. I don't know when it is appropriate to treat students differently, or how to do that, and I don't want to take the risk of making any mistakes in learning to do so."

Being color-blind can also limit educators seeing the many assets and strengths that children of color bring into classrooms and schools via their families and historic backgrounds. Therefore, when educators say they treat all their students the same because that is the fair thing to do, we are concerned because this often means they are not giving students what they need as individuals, which is what we call the practice of equity pedagogy (C. A. M. Banks & Banks, 1995). Besides, working with children and families of color can only help broaden our knowledge and perspectives, making us better professionally and personally because we are exposed to different ways that people make sense of their experiences and view the world. Regarding color-blindness, Milner (2010) states that

> Teachers who adopt a color-blind approach often do not possess the racial knowledge necessary for pedagogical success with diverse students, especially students who are placed on the margins of teaching and learning based on their racialized interactions and experiences inside and outside of the classroom. (p. 121)

Milner (2010) also quotes James Banks (2001) regarding the consequences of educators' maintaining a color-blind approach when Banks wrote:

> A statement such as "I don't see color" reveals a privileged position that refuses to legitimize racial identifications that are very important to people of color and that are often used to justify inaction and perpetuation of the status quo. (2001, p. 12)

We agree with Banks (2001) and Milner (2010) that taking a color-blind approach prevents educators from understanding and including the lived experiences of students of color, and it makes White culture the norm to which all students are compared and judged. Other potential sources of color-blind statements include lack of knowledge about or confidence in discussing inequalities because of race, ethnicity, and language; avoidance of facing potential personal biases; or fear of being judged when taking risks to pursue equity in education. Nevertheless, we believe, as Lisa Delpit (1995) says, "If one does not see color, one does not really see children" (p. 177).

Further, taking a color-blind approach misleads educators regarding the practice of equality versus equity. Students need to be recognized and understood through the lenses by which they and their families are viewed and perceived by the world. To not see color is tantamount to not seeing who students really are and the uniqueness of the cultures they bring to school. At a minimum, readings, discussions, and activities to address the concept of color-blindness should be included in any diversity curriculum. This is especially important because most teachers today are White, female, and monolingual, while most students come from different ethnic, cultural, religious, language, and economic backgrounds (Zumwalt & Craig, 2005).

Cultural conflict. Regarding cultural conflict and issues of power, Milner (2010) makes the case for addressing cultural conflict as foundational to any diversity curriculum because

> When teachers operate mostly or solely from their own cultural references and ways of knowing and experiencing the world, the learning milieu can seem foreign to students of color, students from lower socioeconomic backgrounds, students whose first language is not English, and students who live or have lived in different regions of the country or world. Cultural conflicts in the classroom can result in negative consequences for such students because there are few points of reference and convergence between teachers and students. (p. 122)

Citing Lisa Delpit's (1995) work in describing the culture of power, Milner (2010) discusses the cultural mismatch between students and their teachers as described previously. He also reinforces Delpit's call to explicitly teach students so that they have access to the "language of power" and, therefore, understand the rules and expectations at play both inside and outside today's classrooms. Toward this end, Milner elaborates this point and makes this suggestion:

> Teachers and students should locate common cultural connections to optimize instructional and learning opportunities in social contexts. . . . Knowing what the culture of power actually is, how it works, and how power can be achieved are important conceptual understandings for P–12 student success and should thus be part of both the explicit and implicit curriculum of teacher education. (pp. 122–123)

We agree that confronting issues related to cultural conflict must be a part of every diversity curriculum. Reading Lisa Delpit's (1995) book, as well as other works by such scholars as James Banks, Geneva Gay, bell hooks, Gloria Ladson-Billings, Carol Lee, Sonia Nieto, Christine Sleeter, and others, is one way to do this. Case studies and classic and contemporary videos can be a catalyst for discussions of cultural norms, power, and cultural conflict. These activities are considered "safe" in many multicultural education courses and diversity workshops today, but we believe they may not actually affect the beliefs and dispositions of educators without additional self-reflection and actual experiences in diverse communities.

Myth of meritocracy. Another core concept in any diversity curriculum is confronting what Milner (2010) calls the myth of meritocracy and the role that both white privilege and institutional racism play in perpetuating meritocracy and encouraging deficit-based thinking. Those who believe in meritocracy think that anyone who works hard can live the American Dream and be successful if he just tries hard enough. The truth is that this does not happen for everyone, especially for those who come from communities with poor schools, high unemployment, and a history of being discriminated against and for those who may be recent immigrants or refugees and speak little English. In fact, the myth of meritocracy is obvious in today's economy where citizens who are ready, willing, and able cannot get jobs or get ahead no matter how hard they try. The notion that people can make it if they work hard enough is truly a myth for many, but especially for those from marginalized groups.

White privilege is related to the myth of meritocracy because it offers advantages to some people in our society because light skin color is considered the norm. For example, those of us who are White do not have to think about being followed when we enter a fancy department store or drive through a nice neighborhood, but a young, Black male in these situations might be suspect. White people don't have to think about being denied the chance to rent an apartment or join a country club or apply for certain jobs because of their skin color or their accent. White skin affords many of us unearned privileges that we are not even conscious about and that people of color are often denied or, at least, have to earn, which they are very aware of.

Institutional racism is also connected to the myth of meritocracy and continues to be the legacy of discrimination against people of color regarding policies and practices related to housing, jobs, adequate health care, and education. In other words, while individuals may not discriminate against others, many policies and practices are built into our government, legal, healthcare, and educational institutions that are biased. For example, we still see examples of institutional racism in schools where many students of color are tracked into vocational or tech-prep classes versus honors or advanced placement (AP) classes. In fact, naming the lowest track classes "college-prep" classes in some school systems is a form of institutional racism because not all parents and families realize these classes are the lowest-level classes in the school. Though the name of the class denotes "college prep," many parents are not privy to the fact that AP and international bac-calaureate (IB) classes are weighted more heavily in a student's grade point average (GPA) and college applications than are college prepa-ratory and honors classes. Biased language on standardized tests are another examples of institutional racism that disadvantages some students, as is requiring English Learners (ELs) take the same high-stakes tests as native English speakers within one or two years of entering our school systems.

The myth of meritocracy may be one of the most challenging aspects of a diversity curriculum for many teachers and administra-tors to understand because they do not think about, much less criti-cally examine, how they have been privileged by their educational status, their profession, their socioeconomic status, their race, or their gender. Educators may be completely unaware that they judge others against themselves as being the norm, which leads to believ-ing that if they can make it then everyone can make it if they just try hard enough. Further, their "innocent ignorance" about or their "conscious avoidance" (Cooper, 2007, p. 246) of their beliefs about meritocracy may cause students of color to perceive them negatively. As Lisa Delpit (1995) states, "Those in power are frequently least aware of—or least willing to acknowledge—its existence. Those with less power are often most aware of its existence" (p. 24). For those in power create and maintain the rules for what is and what shall be, just one reason why the myth of meritocracy affects most people of color disproportionately.

As Milner (2010) points out, "The meritocracy argument some-times rejects institutionalized and systemic issues that permeate poli-cies and practices such as racism, sexism, classism, and discrimination both in the classroom and in society" (p. 124), just as does being color-blind. Among other things, meritocracy can lead to students losing their motivation or giving up and dropping out when they feel they cannot succeed because of their color, their lack of English skills, or their status as residents of particular neighborhoods; and many edu-cators think they just aren't trying hard enough. Not recognizing the myth of meritocracy and one's privilege and position as an educator also leads to deficit conceptions, which should be the fourth core con-cept in any diversity curriculum.

Deficit conceptions. Challenging deficit-based thinking is another crucial component of any diversity curriculum. Some examples of deficit-based thinking that we often hear concern parents. We hear, "His parents don't even care if he does his homework or not. They never sign his reading log," and "I can't get her parents to come in for a conference. I've tried several times, and they just don't respond to my notes or phone messages. I don't think they care." When educators assume that parents don't care because they don't send in school supplies or field-trip money or because their child receives free or reduced-priced meals, they make attributions about either the parents or the child based on perceived deficits. If educators assume some students can't achieve academically because of their color, language, shabby clothing, or the neighborhood they come from, they are exhibiting deficit-based thinking. Connecting labels such as limited English proficiency (LEP), English as a second language (ESL), learning disability (LD), or free or reduced meals (FRM) to assumptions about cognitive ability or to perceived gaps in knowledge, skills, or behaviors is deficit-based thinking, which we often find stands in the way of uncovering the strengths of children with such labels. As Milner says,

> Teachers who hold deficit beliefs about students from lower socioeconomic statuses sometimes deliberately avoid including information and skill development in the curriculum. Higher level thinking skills or the skills to critique or analyze content may be purposefully avoided. . . . Deficit conceptions make it difficult for teachers to use what students bring into the learning environment as a place to start and as a place of possibility. While deficit conceptions—can shape teachers' explicit and implicit curriculum—what teachers refuse to cover and include in the curriculum—can also detrimentally shape student learning opportunities. . . . Different from the White majority is sometimes perceived as insufficient, and deficit conceptions manifest in teachers' curriculum practices to the disadvantage of culturally diverse students. (2010, pp. 124–125)

Expectations. The opposite of holding deficit conceptions about people who look or sound different is holding high expectations for all, recognizing the "funds of knowledge" that students bring into the classroom from their families and home communities (Gonzalez, Moll, & Amanti, 2005) and providing the supports needed by each student to be successful in school. Lowering expectations and giving easy work to protect students' self-esteem is naïve at best, and it undermines the purpose of educating students. Furthermore, accepting mediocrity from students, Milner (2010) claims, indicates we do not believe students are capable or do not have the capacity to be successful (p. 125). Dumbing down the curriculum is an easy trap to fall into if educators don't hold high expectations for every student. We believe that not having high expectations for every one of our students is also an issue of social justice.

Resource 1.1 *Milner's (2010) Conceptual Repertoires About Diversity*, which is located on the companion website for this book, provides further details about each of the five conceptual repertoires suggested by Milner (2010). This resource includes typical assertions made by educators about why they may resist these concepts and the instructional consequences of such resistance. We provide this information to assist those who lead discussions about these important topics because acquiring new knowledge about different ways we describe our students; about culturally responsive teaching practices; and about the concepts of color-blindness, cultural conflict, the myth of meritocracy, deficit conceptions, and expectations can be a catalyst for changing our usual ways of thinking about equity and diversity.

Empathy Versus Sympathy

Two additional values guide the development and design of the activities detailed in this book: (1) development of empathy (rather than sympathy) and (2) the use of a strength-based approach. Although it may seem obvious, we want to ensure that educators understand the difference between empathy and sympathy. In our view, empathy is about understanding another's experiences and perspectives well enough to feel that we have walked in their shoes. Being empathetic is experiencing something vicariously—being able to imagine the circumstances and the feelings of others. Sympathy, however, can imply pity or sorrow for others, which often reflects a deficit-based way of thinking about others. We certainly do not want educators to pity our guest speakers, the real-life experiences of the characters portrayed in videos or books, their students, or their students' families and communities. Rather, we want educators to better understand other people's lives through various real-world, and sometimes vicarious, experiences presented later in this book. We want educators to be empathetic so that they will be moved to action but not with shame or disappointment regarding other people's lives. Therefore, we promote a strength-based approach when discussing differences among ourselves, our students, and their families and communities. We consistently make the points that different does not equal bad and that treating people equitably does not mean treating everyone the same. We also work hard to help educators understand that dealing with, enduring through, and overcoming adverse experiences can result in the development of valuable, non-cognitive skills (e.g., leadership), real-life problem solving, and perseverance (Rothstein, 2004). In other words, strength can be derived from adversity, too. We advocate for a strength-based perspective during group discussions, in the presence of guest speakers, during brainstorming sessions, and in case discussions. Strength-based thinking permeates our work, our discussions, and our thinking, and we advocate for this perspective throughout this book

Strength-Based Approach

The strength-based approach we have adopted, which is part of a system of care approach, originally comes from the field of social work (Cross, Bazron, Dennis, & Isaacs, 1989; Saleebey, 1992). For example, we see great strengths in students from low-income neighborhoods who have extended family members or neighbors who look after them when their primary caregiver is working. They are not left on their own, but, instead, they are cared for, fed, helped with homework, and often clothed or housed by their extended family. Further, the local Boys and Girls Club, the neighborhood library, and the family's church community are also assets in their system of care because they serve as supports for the child and the family on many fronts. Such a support network is a real strength for many students, and each aspect of this support network provides an education for children outside of the schoolhouse. They learn important lessons and values from their extended family that may not be recognized in school. For example, they may be resilient, generous to others, or good at problem solving or creative thinking because these are dispositions and skills modeled by their extended family and community.

Educators, especially those interested in working effectively with families and communities, embrace the strength-based approach. A strength-based approach recognizes that all people have strengths, though they have often been untapped or unrecognized. Whether internal or environmental, strengths serve to motivate people toward continued growth (Saleebey, 1992). All children and families have unique talents, skills, and life events that can be used to build, sustain, and maintain communities. For example, students from immigrant and refugee families often learn English more quickly than their parents and serve as translators of both the language and the culture. These students learn very quickly about various transportation, employment, and government systems so they can help their parents access services available to them. How families work through such situations requires strength and skill that can be creatively transferred to school, if teachers, administrators, and schools are aware of them and see them as assets.

Materials and Resources

Textbooks

In typical multicultural education courses or workshops, many excellent reading materials and resources have been used to prepare educators to increase their knowledge and to broaden their thinking about diversity. In the following two sections, we highlight materials we think provide foundational information regarding diversity. We also review commonly used, conventional approaches we have used in professional development workshops related to diversity issues. You can find some textbooks we have used listed in Resource 1.2 *Textbooks Recommended for Learning About Diversity* on this book's companion website.

Historic and Contemporary Videos

Showing excerpts from videos during diversity workshops is another favorite for building background knowledge, especially when there are younger educators for whom the Civil Rights Movement and segregation, for example, are historic events that occurred well before they were born. We have used videos over the years to fill gaps in knowledge or to provide powerful personal, albeit vicarious, experiences with segregation. We use videos because the visual depiction of the lives of people different from ourselves is often a catalyst for decentering our experiences and seems to help develop empathy. Additionally, we ask educators to view newly released or classic full-length videos at home. We then discuss the implicit and explicit messages about the diversity of the characters and the ways they were portrayed on film, always taking a strength-based approach. These discussions occur either face-to-face or online and in small groups because we encourage educators to choose the videos they want to watch rather than have everyone watch the same video. Resource 1.3 *Recommended Videos*, located on this book's companion website, provides a list of videos we have used and recommend for professional development. Although not an exhaustive list, it provides a starting point of readily accessible videos to choose from.

When we debrief videos, we guide educators to acknowledge and critique how the media play out diversity issues. Media portrayals of people's lived experiences should be critiqued carefully from more than one point of view, and many of the questions we discuss with educators push them to take a more critical look at what they viewed. For instance, some videos tend to confirm missionary-zeal beliefs, savior complexes, or great White/Black hope visions. An example of critical reflection prompts for two of the videos we used recently, *Mad Hot Ballroom* and *Akeelah and the Bee,* are provided here to show the types of reflective questions we ask.

Mad Hot Ballroom is an inspiring look inside the lives of New York City school kids on a journey into the world of ballroom dancing, an unexpected arena where they discover new frontiers about attitude, movement, style, and commitment (Officialmoviepage.com, 2010). In this movie, fifth-grade children from low-income families learn ballroom dances, and they compete in a districtwide competition. They learn many lessons through a forum that does not label them with descriptors, Bernice Lott (2001) notes in her literature review on low-income parents/families.

- If learning and the general school experience is all about exposure to the unfamiliar or unthinkable to populations considered at times not worthy, what else could ultimately improve our nation's schools and student achievement?
- Or is lack of exposure another form of *hegemony* (the dominance of one group over other groups, with or without the threat of force, to the extent that, for instance, the dominant party can dictate the terms of trade to its advantage)?
- Why do we make assumptions that others are not interested in middle-class values or cultural capital as deemed important by the powers that be?

How does this movie speak to you and the translation of your beliefs into actions?

Akeelah and the Bee is about a young girl from an inner-city neighborhood who has the phenomenal ability to spell complicated words. She does not realize her ability because of family issues and peer pressure. However, when she does, she dreams *big*. How she evolves in the movie is an example of defying great odds to succeed in areas often assumed that a person like her, from where she comes, and her background, would not often expect. Many messages are shared in this movie.

There are messages about self-esteem, family, community, peer pressure, and teacher expectations, to name a few.

- How does this movie speak to you?
- Have you known any persons like her?
- Have you taught any "Akeelahs" in your teaching experience?
- More important, have you known students like Akeelah and not realized their potential because of their background, who they were, or the like? While you may not admit it about yourself, I am sure that you certainly know colleagues who have done so.
- Did you think that Akeelah's community would respond to her and her plight as they did? After all, she comes from a community where so many people believe that "the parents don't care about their children."
- Have you ever thought that way about the communities of your learners?

Online Learning Resources

One other knowledge-building resource that we use is the IRIS Center materials located online at http://iris.peabody.vanderbilt.edu. This website contains multiple resources including online modules, case studies, interactive activities, information briefs, and podcasts. Some of our favorite resources on this website are the STAR Legacy Modules. We often require educators to complete one or more of these online modules, and then we hold discussions about the content either face-to-face or online. One section of the IRIS Center materials focuses on diversity issues, and there are other materials about accommodations, accountability, assessment, behavior and classroom management, collaboration, content instruction (in math, reading, and writing), differentiation, learning strategies, Response to Intervention (RTI), school improvement, and school leadership. We especially like to assign two of the STAR Legacy modules titled "Cultural and Linguistic Differences: What Teachers Should Know" and "Universal Design for Learning" because they address factors to consider when working with culturally and linguistically diverse students in school settings. Although there is much information in these modules, we usually provide additional readings to supplement the information in each module. For example, with the module called "Cultural and Linguistic Differences: What Teacher Should Know," we usually assign two or three chapters from *Con Respeto* by Guadalupe Valdes to provide additional background knowledge about Mexican-heritage families. We also develop higher-order discussion questions, even though there are thought questions provided at the start of each module and assessment questions at the end.

Guest Speakers

We often use guest speakers as another resource because they can talk personally about issues with which we are not familiar or have not experienced ourselves. Choosing guest speakers has been very successful, especially when the group members are the same age, speak the same language, or are from the same profession as the presenters. Seeing and hearing from people with firsthand experience is much more powerful for developing empathy and for seeing how a strength-based approach actually works rather than reading about the same experience. For example, we ask professional educators who are gay, lesbian, bisexual, or transgendered to discuss how they experience being different from the rest of the people with whom they work, as well as from most parents. We also ask parents of students with disabilities, as well as students who are living with disabilities, to speak about their or their children's experiences with school. Panels of presenters always seem to be better received than does a single presenter because of the range of perspectives they bring to the topic. Panels of guest speakers may be even more powerful than reading books or seeing videos because the audience can ask questions of guest speakers. Further, hearing authentic voices provides them with information about their lived experiences, debunks many stereotypes, sometimes engenders empathy, and often serves as a catalyst to do more for marginalized students and their families. Finally, listening to others' experiences helps educators better understand what not to do, say, or allow in their classrooms. In other words, panel members are experts of their lived experiences and become our teachers, offering ways we can most effectively teach and reach students in similar, yet different circumstances.

Other Commonly Used Activities and Approaches

The resources mentioned previously engage educators in thinking and learning about diversity, and help them gain cultural competence. As teacher educators and professional development facilitators, we have also used other approaches or activities to encourage active participation in the learning process. Some of the more traditional approaches we have used are described in the next section. While these activities take place mainly inside the school, activities we use that take educators' learning outside of school are described in later chapters, as we discuss developing critical cultural competence.

Nevertheless, discussions and reflections are something we use regularly in all our diversity workshops.

Discussions and Reflection

Reflection has long been advocated in the literature as a vital means of investigating the personal and professional self (Schmidt, 1999; Schön, 1996; Zeichner, 1993), and we find that discussion is most useful when it takes place after educators have had a chance to think about and reflect on what they have read, seen, or experienced. Through various opportunities for reflection, educators recognize how and why they have come to believe as they do about people who are different from them or the issues raised in readings, videos, and discussions they have with others.

Even when we introduce a new topic, we often begin by having educators reflect in writing or orally in discussion with peers (which we call sometimes call base groups, talking partners, or learning pods). For example, we might ask them to define what they think the differences are between race, ethnicity, and culture. Or we may ask for their written reactions to an article they read about the social construction of race and ethnicity (Applebaum, 2003; Jewett, 2006; Khanna & Harris, 2009) prior to discussing this topic with peers in small or large groups. Alternatively, we might lead a brainstorming session to generate words associated with topics, such as sex and gender, ageism, or students with disabilities, purposefully to uncover the range of associations, beliefs, and ideas and to acknowledge any prior knowledge about the topic. For example, in our initial sessions on diverse learners, we write on the board every term that participants associate with the concept of culture. Words are very powerful carriers of our feelings and understandings about different concepts, as well as expressions of our biases and stereotypes. Therefore, we purposefully choose potentially controversial terms, such as "affirmative action" or "meritocracy" or "White privilege" to promote reflection on educators' beliefs about these topics.

Sometimes we do these brainstorming exercises in online forums, either synchronously in chat rooms or on a wiki, or asynchronously using blogs or discussion boards. When educators are asked to respond to one another, whether face-to-face or in online forums, we often find they can teach one another, sometimes better than we can. However, expressions of one's beliefs and feelings may include stereotypes and biases. If the goal is not only to increase knowledge and self-knowledge but also to develop critical cultural competence, we have found that a combination of public and private self-reflection has been more effective than one or the other. Public statements have the advantage of allowing (and sometimes requiring) people to justify themselves to others, but not everyone is brave enough to express her beliefs in public. Private opportunities for written reflection, by contrast, offer opportunities to reveal one's beliefs without the fear of being judged. However, we recognize that some educators may mask their private beliefs in politically correct language in any context. In such cases, reflection as a means of helping educators become more self-aware may not immediately be visible, and may require feedback from a skillful facilitator to challenge and, perhaps, advance the perceptions of some.

In our experience, however, reflection by itself is insufficient for increasing critical cultural competence, thus, multiple experiences and opportunities followed by public and private reflection are necessary for developing critical cultural competence. New and experienced educators need to read, view videos, and listen to guest speakers to increase their knowledge base and to fill in gaps in their experience and understanding. They also need to uncover, confront, and address their personal beliefs and misconceptions. Discussion along with reflection adds value by requiring that educators explain their thinking. This is a crucial step. Similarly, we know change cannot happen unless the context for discussion and reflection feels safe to participants. Therefore, we establish norms with each group about active listening and respectful disagreement, and we model these behaviors at all times. Sometimes, we repeat back what we hear; sometimes, we ask what others think. We have also learned to handle controversy when something someone says crosses the line for another person in the group. And we learn from each group of educators we encounter.

Case Studies and Case Discussions

In addition to using textbooks, videos, online materials, and guest speakers to help educators develop their knowledge base, build empathy, and better understand social justice issues, we also use case studies to build self-knowledge and empathy and to practice taking a strength-based approach. The personal nature of the stories of real individuals in case studies and vignettes seems to allow people to decenter and focus on the issues in the case. At the same time, cases can be catalysts for educators reflecting about how they might respond personally to the case if they were in a similar situation. We usually take a problem-solving approach while discussing cases, although there are many purposes for using cases. Most often, we try to separate the facts of the case from the inferences we make about the people and situations in the case and then move on to naming the issues in the case and explaining importance to us as teachers, administrators, or parents. Next, we select specific issues or problems from the case and brainstorm potential solutions. As the facilitators of a case discussion, we always try to remind the participants to take a strength-based, rather than deficit, approach when trying to find solutions to the issues identified in the case. We also remind educators to apply any readings, videos, or personal experiences to the issues in the cases. Finally, we discuss the pros and cons of each potential solution, once again trying to take a strength-based perspective. Because there is no one right answer to the problems raised by any particular case, we also try to prioritize solutions or determine their short-term or long-term application.

Book Clubs

As much as we find textbooks and articles to be valuable resources, we find that many educators are more motivated by and interested in reading other kinds of books. One tried–and-true activity we use to increase cultural competence is book clubs. We usually offer several choices for a book club reading because we know that having choices is motivating. Once participants have made their book club selection from a group of recommended books, we conduct book club discussions in several different ways. Over the years, some of these include small groups reading the same book and meet face-to-face several times for discussion. This strategy operates similarly to literature circles used in schools (Daniels, 2002; Harvey & Goudvis, 2007). Usually, each book club group sets the amount of reading to be completed for each of these discussions and is self-directed during its discussions. Sometimes, we suggest participants take roles in their book clubs to experience what it might be like to do book clubs or literature circles with students. For example, sometimes, they take turns being the discussion director, the connection maker, the summarizer, the word wizard, or the passage picker (Raphael, 1994). We have also used online discussions among book club members with good success, and we think professional learning communities (PLCs) are ideal groups with which to engage in book club discussions. Finally, we have been especially successful with book club when using a jigsaw approach to reading both books and articles or chapters.

ACTIVITY 1.1 BOOK CLUB JIGSAW ACTIVITY

Objectives

- To read books related to cultural diversity
- To represent our understanding of the book using graphic organizers
- To share our thoughts through reflections and discussions

Instruction to Participants

Have participants select a book from the list located in Resource 1.4 *Book Club List* on this book's companion website. Group the participants based on the book they select from the list you provide. Participants meet to discuss their book with those who have read the same book. Then they meet at a different time in new groups where everyone has read a different book and serves as expert for this book. Experts share what they learned from and what they liked or disliked about the book they read. In our book clubs, we also ask each person to create some kind of graphic or graphic organizer to represent visually the most important parts of their book. We find that requiring visual representations of the content and of the most important messages in their books forces most educators to think outside the box because they have to use more than words to represent their book. Teachers and administrators are very creative, and their graphic representations can be completed by hand or by using a computer, whichever they prefer. Copies of their graphics representations are then provided to other jigsaw group members, who have not read that book, as handouts. These representations serve as talking points for the book expert and as references for future reading by others in the jigsaw groups. An example of a book club graphic is provided in Resource 1.5 *Book Club Graphics* for Train Go Sorry *by Leah Hager Cohen* on this book's companion website so you can provide an example to those in your professional development sessions.

Games and Simulations

Games and simulations, such as Barnga and BaFa BaFa, or the version of Monopoly described later, are excellent catalysts for discussing how diversity impacts cross-cultural communication and other topics related to developing critical cultural competence. We sometimes play Barnga (Thiagarajan, 2006), which serve as a simulation of cross-cultural communication for understanding cultural clashes and ESL students' experiences. Barnga is a card game where different groups of people play cards with one another using different rules at each table. The trick is that players are not allowed to communicate orally at any time during or between games. Once the participants in each group have played a few rounds based on the rules they were given, winners and losers move to different groups and start playing again—still without talking. However, in these new groups, players are playing with different rules, so they have to figure out how they are going to play together under these new circumstances, and conflicts start to occur. How various players handle themselves when the rules have changed is important to process when the allotted time is up. As with all games and simulations, the discussion afterward deserves serious time and needs to be planned by the group leader so that discussion moves beyond personal experience of the game to explore the underlying issues related to cultural diversity.

Other games and simulations can offer similar experiences to people involved, although they may be more complex and take more time to play than Barnga. BaFa BaFa, for example, is a simulation that helps participants better understand how different groups approach common aspects of culture, such as ways of communicating, personal space, gender interactions, relationships between superiors and subordinates, and rules that guide social interactions. In BaFa BaFa, participants are placed in two different "cultural" groups with different sets of rules and expectations, and then they interact with the other group over an hour or so. Visitors and observers who only understand their norms then try to figure out how to trade successfully with the other cultural group. Resulting missteps, misperceptions, and stereotypes experienced by the participants become the basis for debriefing about the impact of cultural norms on our interactions in a multicultural society.

The Game of Monopoly

Objective

- To experience vicariously inequities such as racism, privilege, institutional racism by playing a modified version of Monopoly

Instruction to Participants

Another game we use in multicultural education classes and diversity workshops is a version of Monopoly that provides players with a "metaphorical explanation of issues of racism, institutional racism, and White privilege" (Jost, Whitfield, & Jost, 2005, p. 16). The rules of the traditional game of Monopoly are slightly modified, including the number of actual players and the inclusion of volunteers. Typically, six to eight players are needed, which includes a volunteer banker and a volunteer observer. This version of Monopoly is a great learning activity because it allows active engagement with societal issues and actions that are realities for some groups and unrealities for others. The only change in rules is

(Continued)

(Continued)

that while two players start the game, two more don't enter the game until 30 to 40 minutes later (or after five to seven rounds), and two more players enter the game another 30 to 40 minutes after that (or after another five to seven rounds).

Recommended Questions Following the Activity (I=Individual Reflection Questions, G=Group Discussion Questions)

It is important to note, however, that for real understanding to occur prior preparation for playing this version of Monopoly should include reading about the history of dominated cultures (Jost et al., 2005). It is important for educators to understand, for example, historic inequities in education for students of color, affirmative action policies, institutional racism, the achievement gap, and White privilege. After the game, the players' insights must be shared, processed, and deconstructed. However, the game as a metaphor of racial inequities in schools and society, affirmative action, and privilege must be unveiled if the players don't explicitly state it themselves. Instructions recommended for debriefing this game with the whole group can be found in Resource 1.6 *Debriefing the Game of Monopoly* on this book's companion website.

Other reflection questions following games and simulations like Barga, BaFa BaFa, or this version of Monopoly can include the following:

- What did you learn about yourself participating in this game/simulation? (I, G)
- What did you learn about other people who participated with you? (I, G)
- In what ways does this the purpose of this game/simulation relate to the development of critical cultural competence? (I, G)

Empathy Activities

In past workshops and classes, we have included what we call empathy activities like the trust walk or blind walk. This activity is done with one partner blindfolded and the other partner responsible for helping the "blind" person navigate safely in a classroom, a school, or the community. We have also had educators experience what it might be like to be in wheelchair to get around and to have a sight or hearing impairment. By putting educators in groups with one in a wheelchair, one with petroleum jelly smeared on his glasses or blindfolded, and with one wearing earplugs, we send them out to run errands at certain locations so that they can begin to empathize with the struggles many people with disabilities face every day. Of course, the limitation of this exercise is that participants can get out of the wheelchair anytime they want, take off the glasses, and remove the earphones. Therefore, participants only get a glimpse of what it must be like to have a disability for less than an hour of their life. As a result, this activity by itself (as most of the activities in this book) has limited use when done in singly or in isolation from other activities. Yet it raises awareness and can be a catalyst for deeper discussions about abilities and disabilities. And although we often ask guest speakers with motor or visual disabilities to help us debrief these kinds of activities and to demonstrate a particular disability in a more realistic manner, these activities have limited use.

We have tried other ways to develop deeper awareness, knowledge, and empathy for other struggles that the families of students in our schools experience by extending some empathy awareness activities to last for up to seven days. For example, we have asked educators to choose and engage in one of the following activities:

- Take only public transportation for one week
- Eat on $5 per day for a week
- Wear the same clothes for a week
- Live on a budget of $100 a week to include all food, transportation, shelter, clothing, and entertainment

Once again, debriefing is key so that the result is the development of empathy, and not sympathy, for those less privileged. Reflection on these events indicates that they serve as a positive step in the direction of developing cultural competence but are not sufficient in and of themselves. Therefore, in later chapters, we discuss some community adventures we have developed and used with educators to develop empathy. We do this because in our experience more personal experience with families and in the community is needed to develop critical cultural competence beyond engagement with the common resources and activities discussed in this chapter. We believe the kinds of activities that get teachers and administrators out of their comfort zone and out of their classrooms or schools and into the community, which most of the activities described in this chapter do not, are needed to move from cultural awareness to cultural competence and finally to critical cultural competence. Therefore, in upcoming chapters we focus in more depth on the three key elements for developing critical cultural competence: understanding of self, students, and parents and communities.

SUMMARY OF KEY POINTS

In this chapter, we reviewed typical goals often used in multicultural education and diversity workshops and described in more detail several core concepts and values that undergird the kinds of activities for developing critical cultural competence presented throughout this book. In addition, we described resources and activities that are commonly used in diversity workshops as ways to develop foundational knowledge. However, in this book we strive to go beyond knowledge and to provide activities to develop educators with critical cultural competence.

- Richard Milner (2010) suggested that that developing a deep and complex understanding of the five conceptual repertoires should be the common core for any diversity curriculum. These concepts include (1) color-blindness, (2) cultural conflict, (3) the myth of meritocracy, (4) deficit conceptions, and (5) expectations. In this book, we share ideas to challenge educators in these five repertoires, build empathy, and enable them to use a strength-base approach in their work in the diverse communities within and beyond school settings.
- Resources and materials including textbooks, videos, online resources, guest speakers, and additional readings are shared to support further discussions and to engage educators in critical thinking and reflection.
- Commonly used approaches including discussions and reflections, book clubs, case studies and case discussions, simulation and other games, and empathy-development activities are also shared.

REFLECTION AND EXTENSION

Reflecting on your experiences attending or leading diversity courses and workshops, answer the following

- What are the resources and materials you have used with good success?
- What are some of your favorite and most engaging activities?
- What are the most challenging questions you hear from educators?

ONLINE EXTENSIONS

When we teach online versions of our multicultural education courses and diversity workshops, we often use a wiki for brainstorming everything the participants think they know about a topic such as culture, to compare their thoughts on race and ethnicity, or find their associations with the words "gender" and "sexual orientation." We do this before further readings about or discussion of these topics, and then we collect all the words from our brainstorming on the wiki (or sometimes from the saved script of a live chat) and put them into an online program like Wordle or WordSift. These free tools found on the Internet create word clouds or tag clouds that sort and display the words so that the most frequently used words show up as the most prominent in a collage of all the words submitted. The results are then shared with the group to elicit further reflection and discussion. The content of any text, web page, blog, wiki, chat room, and so on can be cut and pasted into Wordle or Wordsift to provide a visual representation of the prominent, and perhaps most important, words in that text. Although the results can be surprising at times, these tools offer the opportunity to visualize what the discussion of a particular topic emphasized. In addition, Wordle.com and, especially, WordSift.com both have some additional features that teachers find useful in other contexts than our online workshops. These features can be especially useful in assisting ELs with learning key vocabulary in the various texts they have to compre-hend. What you see next is the results of pasting the entire text of this chapter into WordSift.com and sorting the words from rare to common. As you can see, the most prominent words used in this chapter include *student, educator, book, teacher, diversity,* and *discussion.*

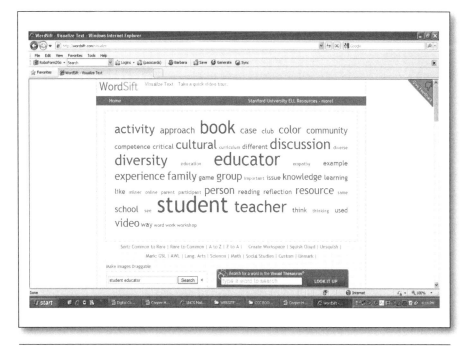

Created by Dr. Kenji Hakuta, Stanford University.

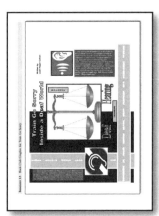

2

Who I Am

How Can We Understand Ourselves as Cultural Beings?

Introduction

When the goal is to help educators develop critical cultural competence, we must begin by using strategies that go beyond knowledge about others to include self-knowledge. Educators must be able to answer the question, *Who am I as a teacher?* or *Who am I as an administrator?* The activities described in this chapter aim to help educators better understand themselves as cultural beings and to provide multiple opportunities to analyze and reflect on their identities as multifaceted cultural beings. Toward this end, we describe many activities that we have used to invite educators to uncover, reflect on, and reveal both their public and private identities. We use these activities as a foundation for better understanding the many assets that students bring to the classroom. We believe that knowing one's self as a complex, cultural being has to come before educators can begin to appreciate the diversity of today's students, their families, and communities.

Exploring Personal Characteristics and Beliefs

Answering the question, *Who am I as an educator?* is not a simple task, nor can it be accomplished by completing some activities or reflections during a few professional development sessions. First, it isn't easy because educators play many roles in their schools and districts. They may be surrogate mothers or fathers, counselors, nurses, coaches, judges, leaders, and more depending on what students need. Their professional identity encompasses many roles. Educators also lead complex lives and take on many identities in addition to that of professional educator. They may be husband/wife, parent, grandparent, amateur gardener, community leader, fitness fanatic, and so on. Second, culture itself is not simple concept. In fact, many White, female teachers tell us that they don't have any culture because they understand culture as being about others, including minority groups, foreigners, or immigrants. They also deny having a culture because of the issue of White privilege discussed in the previous chapter. They speak English only; they are not connected to the cultures of their ancestors; they have not been discriminated against; and they don't see themselves as different from what they perceive as mainstream culture. For these reasons, we select from the activities suggested in this chapter to help teachers and administrators discover and reflect more deeply on who they are as cultural beings. Some of these activities, like writing an autobiography or one's philosophy of education, are common activities that many educators may have done previously, but they are good places to begin the process of developing critical cultural competence.

Other activities we recommend, such as doing various All About Me activities or creating A Picture of Me poster, for example, ask educators to use different media and go beyond the written word to express who they are as cultural beings. However, we *always* define culture *before* we ask educators to consider how they self-identify regarding many aspects of culture, which may include, but are not limited to, their race, ethnicity, primary language or dialect, gender, sexual orientation, religious beliefs, ability or disability, occupation, geographic identity, age/generation, affiliations or identification with various organizations, hobbies/interests, position or role in their family, and the like. In fact, we often use the image of an iceberg or the layers of an onion as metaphors to describe which aspects of culture are visible to others and how the depth and complexity of a person's cultural identity can be revealed only by looking below the surface or peeling away the layers of the onion. These metaphors also help us make the point that identity is not just how we perceive ourselves but also about how we are perceived by others.

Although many people have defined culture in more or less complex ways over the years, we always begin by developing a definition of culture together with those in our diversity workshops. Sometimes, we get into debates about what culture is; if there is an American culture and what it is; whether culture resides in individuals or in groups; and how we can describe and deal with multiple, coexisting identities and cultures in our lives as we try to coconstruct a robust definition of culture. With the goal of developing critical cultural competence we also discuss (1) the dynamic and changing nature of culture; (2) how culture is formed, maintained, and changed; and (3) how self-identification as a cultural being has political, social, and, perhaps, economic consequences. For example, revealing oneself as a Black, female, Christian, single, gay kindergarten teacher may have a very different impact on others than revealing one's identity as a high school English teacher who is a White, Jewish, middle-aged, and the father of four teenage sons.

Also, it is very important to note that all discussions of who I am as a professional educator and how I understand and reveal my cultural identity to others must happen only when respect has been established and safety is assured. The facilitator must model respectful behavior and insist on it during all discussions of culture and identity, especially when educators share publicly rather than just write privately about one's self. Most leaders of professional development are skilled in leading discussions, understanding group dynamics, and turning potential misunderstandings or conflicts into learning experiences. Nevertheless, we suggest using the guidelines for group leaders, as well as for the participants in group discussions provided by Everyday Democracy (www.everyday-democracy.org), which we have included in Resource 2.1 *Suggestions for Leading and Participating in Democratic Discussions* on this book's companion website. These guidelines can be used as they are, but we think it preferable for the facilitator to develop group norms for safe and civil discussions *with* each group of educators before processing, sharing, or debriefing any activities in this book.

Both public and private reflections on who I am as a teacher or administrator are worthwhile, but our experience is that the learning is greater for everyone when discussions of self, identity, and culture are public because others' perceptions are also important to how we understand ourselves. In fact, we believe that to develop critical cultural competence, educators need to enhance their self-knowledge and learn to reveal their beliefs and values appropriately in interactions with peers, students, and families. Further, we believe that critical cultural competence requires being effective in cross-cultural communication, and one place to begin is to learn how, when, and to what extent we should reveal our cultural background to others.

Next, we describe several activities to help educators explore and express their personal characteristics and beliefs. These include writing autobiographies and educational philosophies, as well as engaging in a variety of different All About Me activities. While many activities can be reconfigured and used by teachers to learn more about their K–12 students, the instructions we provide are meant for use with adults in professional development settings. Additional activities follow that aim to help educators reveal their beliefs and identities in more public ways. These include participation in an intercultural scavenger hunt to learn about others in their professional learning communities (PLCs) or in a variety of other professional development settings, the creation and sharing of Bio-Poems, and participation in the Privilege Walk activity. Some activities are ways to express the cultural identity we want others to see and are willing to reveal, while others are about expressing the cultural identities we want to believe we have. Still other activities reveal who we are but do not want others to see. In all cases, these activities can be used to emphasize self-knowledge because such knowledge is a first step toward developing critical cultural competence.

ACTIVITY 2.1 AUTOBIOGRAPHIES

In our diverse world, understanding one's cultural identity and being more open to others is an extremely important habit of mind for educators to possess. Autobiographies are a good place for teachers and administrators to begin critically reflecting about themselves as cultural beings because they investigate the person they know best—themselves. Writing autobiographies asks educators to explicitly describe their lives, usually, in a factual sense, and can be used to better understand one's self and answer the question, Who am I as an educator?

Autobiographies are usually written chronologically, but they can also have a specific focus such as educators' lived experiences as readers, with mathematics, or of the motivation to become a teacher or administrator. However, for developing critical cultural competence, we encourage educators to write about their experiences with diversity as young children, as school-age and college-age students, as adults, and as professionals. The autobiography activities described later are what we consider cultural autobiographies, and are different from traditional autobiographies that chronologically narrate one's life. Instead, they are designed to reveal one's identity as a cultural being based on personal assumptions and remembrances. If written thoughtfully, such cultural autobiographies can reveal preconceived assumptions relative to the various microcultures or subgroups that make up one's cultural identity and perceived place in society. Writing a cultural autobiography is intended to help educators understand the complexity of the self as a cultural being.

Autobiographies should be based on facts, but there is no way to check this, and sometimes, what is perceived as factual may be a vague or mistaken remembrance of long-ago experiences that now seem factual. This is not important for writing a cultural autobiography because perception is reality for most of us. However, when it comes to sharing cultural autobiographies publicly, discussing them, and, perhaps, answering questions in a group, we always allow educators to decide if they are comfortable sharing all or a portion of their autobiography. Additionally, as the group leaders, we always model by sharing a portion of our cultural autobiography.

Sometimes, we use the cultural autobiography activity described next, and sometimes, we use Resource 2.2 *Alternative Autobiographical Sketch* described in this book's companion. If time is short, we at least recommend discussing each of the questions in Resource 2.2, one at a time, with members of your PLC or in other small-group sessions.

Objective

- To provide participants with an opportunity to share how they perceive themselves in relation to aspects of culture that situate them as cultural beings, and to explore one's own cultural assumptions

Instruction to Participants

Think and write about how you identify with each of the following aspects of culture: gender/sexual orientation, ethnicity, race, class, geography, age, exceptionality (abilities and/or disabilities), socioeconomic status, religion, and language. Also, feel free to write additional aspects of culture that may be important to you such as your family members, occupation, hobbies, personal or family values, customs, and the like.

Begin with the aspect of culture that currently has the most impact on you as an educator, and work down to what you perceive to be the least influential aspect of culture influencing you.

Take each aspect of culture one at a time, explain how your membership in a particular subgroup has helped create both the kind of person and the kind of educator you are now or want to become.

(Continued)

(Continued)

Recommended Questions Following the Activity (I=Individual Reflection Questions, G=Group Discussion Questions)

- In what ways do your experiences with various cultural subgroups influence how you identify yourself to others? (I, G)
- In what ways do your experiences with various cultural subgroups influence your relationships with others who identify with different cultural subgroups? (G)
- In what ways do your experiences with various cultural subgroups influence your personality? (I, G)
- In what ways do you think the sharing of your experiences will impact how others may receive, perceive, or believe you as an educator? (I, G)

Time

- It is estimated to take one to three hours for writing, plus time for each person in the group to share.

One final thought about cultural autobiographies, as educators become more savvy with technology, or when they want to assign an autobiography to their students, we highly recommend the use of video and other graphic images to enrich the presentation of one's cultural autobiography. And while we recommend several free Internet programs when we describe how to create culture posters, we also encourage teachers and their students to consider using image-editing software such as Apple's iMovie, Microsoft's PhotoStory 3 or MovieMaker, Adobe's Premiere, and even PowerPoint for creating and sharing cultural autobiographies. Adding multimedia (photos, graphics, video, music, text, and narration) when creating autobiographies can be motivating but time consuming. Nevertheless, it is a viable option for 21st-century educators and students, and several examples of cultural autobiographies can be found on YouTube.

ACTIVITY 2.2 EDUCATIONAL PHILOSOPHY

Writing one's philosophy of education is another commonly used activity that helps educators develop self-awareness and metacognitive understanding of their educational beliefs, which we believe will help educators develop critical cultural competence. Teacher and administrator beliefs and values about teaching, learning, students, curriculum, and schooling guide how they act and what they do. Educational philosophies can and should be used to help new and experienced educators reflect critically with the goal of continuous improvement throughout their careers. However, with the goal of developing educators with critical cultural competence, writing their philosophies focuses on their attitudes, beliefs, values, and goals for meeting the needs of diverse students. We also encourage them to include concrete examples and/or stories so that we don't get just platitudes and vague, general statements such as "I believe that all children can learn." Typically, we ask educators to develop their teaching philosophy as described later, but we also provide the questions described Resource 2.3 *Questions to Help You Develop Your Educational Philosophy* on this book's companion website. Once again, if time is short, these questions can be discussed in a PLC or other small-group setting.

Objective

- To provide participants with an opportunity to reveal how their philosophy of education, including their attitudes, beliefs, values, and goals for meeting the needs of diverse students, guides their actions and interactions with students, parents, and the community

Instruction to Participants

Please address the following topics in your philosophy of education: your attitudes, beliefs, values, and goals regarding (a) your learners, (b) your roles as an educator, (c) the curriculum and instruction, (d) parents and families, and (e) the school community. In addition, you may want to address your attitudes, beliefs, values, and goals regarding topics such as classroom management, differentiation, assessment, motivation, specific instructional strategies, collaboration, technology, professional development, reflection, and meeting the needs of diverse groups of students (i.e., students who tend to perform poorly in content areas, inclusion students, ethnic minority students, teaching boys versus girls, English Learners, etc.).

Please be sure to elaborate on why and how you have come to believe each part of your educational philosophy. Don't stop at just stating your philosophy. Make it personal by including as many concrete examples and/or stories as possible in your educational philosophy.

Please avoid making statements that are vague or so general that they sound like platitudes.

Write in the first person. Avoid writing about what other educators should believe, value, think, or do. Write about what *you* believe, value, think, and do.

Recommended Questions Following the Activity (I=Individual Reflection Questions, G=Group Discussion Questions)

- How has your educational philosophy changed over time? What do you think has influenced those changes? (I)

(Continued)

(Continued)

- What aspects of your educational philosophy influence your practice the most often? (I)
- What aspects are you still working on making a part of your regular practice? (I)
- What aspects do you have in common with others in your PLC or discussion partner/group? (G)
- What aspects are you able to enact in your practice? What supports you to be able to enact these aspects of your philosophy? (G)
- What aspects are you not able to enact in your practice? Why? (G)

Time

- Depending on the suggested length of the teaching philosophy (1–2 pages or 5–6 pages), the time to write for most educators will vary from one to three hours. Time for sharing and discussion is also needed because we think the value of this activity is in the sharing as much as in the writing.

ACTIVITY 2.3 ALL ABOUT ME ACTIVITIES

Other ways to expand educators' self-knowledge and to help them answer the question of who they are include numerous All About Me activities. Some of these activities are quick, easy, and fun, but they are not always effective for moving educators toward critical cultural competence because they are usually used as icebreakers or to build community. Nevertheless, we briefly describe several All About Me activities because they provide additional resources for professional development; educators have enjoyed doing them and have found them helpful with their students. The times vary for completing each of these activities, and most activities require the participants to do a little homework. Therefore, we select All About Me activities according to the grade levels represented in workshops, the time we have available for professional development, and our goals.

Objective

- To provide participants with an opportunity to explore various aspects of their identity and share them publicly with others

Family oral history. Sharing a family story is a great way to reveal a part of one's heritage and, therefore, one's culture. Most educators love to tell stories, making this is a great All About Me activity. Stories about one's family history can be shared spontaneously; they can be researched, written, and shared later, and they can focus on a specific theme for exploring and sharing specific aspects of culture. We often read a piece of children's literature to spark thinking about family stories. For example, with elementary teachers, we use Patricia Pollacco's stories for helping educators choose stories to share that are a part of their autobiography *and* convey a sense of importance to the aspects of their culture and family heritage. Often, we ask educators to bring an artifact that represents their family's cultural heritage or the history of their family. Many people bring photographs, but many others bring actual artifacts that represent their family heritage. Of course, we model by sharing one of our family stories or artifacts so that everyone understands the purpose these activities. Also, sharing important aspects of our lives with our groups tends to take away the "student and teacher" feeling and engenders an "us" dynamic; in other words, by sharing we, too, become a part of the learning community. We ask the group to reflect on the value of family oral history for better understanding the depth and breadth of each person's cultural identity, and we find that many teachers take the concept of family stories and oral history back to their classrooms to use as writing or speaking activities. Sharing their family oral history, educators grasp the importance of incorporating family and cultural backgrounds in their classrooms and schools. When teachers make the time to do activities such as these with their students, they begin the process of becoming more culturally responsive as well.

Quilt squares. Another All About Me activity is to ask everyone to create one square that, along with quilt squares from other participants, will make up a quilt. We do this simply by giving each participant a 9- × 9-inch square of construction paper and asking them to decorate a quilt square to represent themselves as individuals. Alternatively, we ask them to decorate their quilt square to represent their family's heritage or their cultural background. We usually ask educators to do this activity at home so they have access to things like photographs, magazines to cut from, computers, markers or crayons, and other items from which they can design their quilt square. The fun part is when they bring their quilt squares back to the next session and share their identity or their family's culture by describing everything they have added to their quilt square.

When participants finish sharing and answering any questions from the group, we piece together the quilt and hang it on the wall for display during our time together. The image of the completed quilt pieced together from individual contributions is a great metaphor for talking about the mosaic that makes up our diverse classrooms today. In fact, we often end this activity by talking about why the metaphor of our society as a melting pot is outdated and inappropriate because we cannot see the value of individual contributions to our society from all different cultures if they are blended together into one pot. Instead, we discuss the pros and cons of several other metaphors for our diverse society, including that of a beautiful patchwork quilt made of squares of such variety.

ABC books. Sometimes, we ask educators to create an ABC book about their family and cultural background. ABC books are usually full of images and have

(Continued)

(Continued)

brief captions on each page indicating how each image and each letter of the alphabet is All About Me. Participants who prefer a more creative outlet for sharing their background and interests often opt for an ABC book rather than an autobiography. During sharing time, when they read their ABC book to the group, they often elaborate on the choices they made for each page to represent their family and cultural heritage. Educators reach the same level of reflection about their cultural identity by doing this activity as they do when writing their autobiography or telling a family oral history story, so we often offer any of these activities as choices among several possible All About Me activities.

Many teachers have their students create ABC books or do other types of All About Me books with specific pages for a self-portrait, and for sharing their family, where they live, what activities they enjoy doing, among many other ideas. Elementary teachers often do these activities at the start of the school year to get to know their students and to assess what their skills are in writing, spelling, and drawing. And while we have no problems with students creating All About Me books, we encourage educators to make these less superficial and try to modify them so that students can really learn more about family and cultural heritage. Simply having students draw and, perhaps, write about with whom they live can be very insightful for educators, as long as they take the time to talk with each student about whom and what makes up their drawing. Most educators are quite sensitive now to the diversity of families and don't make the mistake of asking children to create traditional family trees. Instead, as with the activity described next, they ask their students to explain with whom they live and discuss whom they consider family with the goal of learning as much as they can about their students.

Name stories. Paul Gorski describes an activity he calls name stories at www .edchange.org/multicultural/activities/name.html, which is very similar to an activity that we also use to discuss with educators how important names are to students. Like Paul Gorski, in our activity, we ask educators to (1) tell us how they received each part of their names, (2) what they prefer to be called, (3) an explanation of any nicknames they have, and (4) what their names means, if anything, and where they come from—if they know. Although we often ask everyone in our groups to share the origins of their names early in our time together, we sometimes do this in small groups, starting with partners and then moving into groups of four where each person introduces a partner to the group of four and explains the origins of the partner's name. Sometimes, we double the size of the group again so there are eight people in a group, and each person is responsible for explaining his or her partner's name story to new members of the group. This activity promotes active listening and begins to generate comfort in the group as everyone gets to know one another better. These kinds of activities are useful when PLCs are first starting as well. Most important, when we debrief this activity, we discuss the importance of getting the names of their students and their students' family names correct. We suggest doing so by making the time to ask about their names, how to pronounce them, if they have a particular meaning, and who gave them their name. We also suggest that rather than calling out names, they ask students to tell them their names so they hear the correct pronunciation first. This practice not only reduces embarrassment when we mispronounce a name or fail to use a nickname a student prefers, but it also models respect for students. Although this may not be something that White, middle-class, monolingual teachers feel is important, it is very important to students and indicates educators developing a sense of cultural competence. Many other name games can be used as warm-ups and community-building activities, and we referenced Paul Gorski's version of this activity because it helps build intercultural understanding and respect through sharing and recognizing one aspect of people's cultural identities. Several other excellent awareness activities that we highly recommend can be found the EdChange website at www.edchange .org/multicultural/activityarch.html.

Me bags and treasure boxes. One more All About Me activity that we use asks educators to decorate a simple paper lunch bag to show aspects of their personal and cultural identities. They can draw on the bag, which we provide; use words or pictures cut from magazines; or print computer graphics to decorate their bags. We also ask them to put one or more artifacts into their me bags to represent themselves, their interests, or their cultural values to share with their peers. We sometimes do something very similar using shoeboxes or any relatively small box with a lid that we call treasure boxes to represent their *treasured* heritage. Sometimes, we bring a backpack or a small suitcase full of items that represent our cultural heritage and to model the kinds of artifacts that might go into their me bag or treasure box. We believe the simple process of decorating the outside and selecting artifacts for a me bag or a treasure box to represent family heritage and cultural identities are steps toward developing cultural competence because they require reflection and self-knowledge. The process, we believe, is more important than the product, but nonetheless, it is important that sharing and discussion following any of these All About Me activities. We do not want to lose the point of doing something fun and creative if the goal is to begin to develop critical cultural competence.

Recommended Questions Following All About Me Activities (I=Individual Reflection Questions, G=Group Discussion Questions)

- What did you learn about yourself while doing this project? (I)
- What did you find yourself wanting to share publicly and wanting to keep private? (I)
- What can you learn about your students by doing some of these activities with them? What will still be unknown to you? (G)

(Continued)

(Continued)

- What are the benefits and/or the drawbacks of using any of these activities with your students?
- What are some ways to modify the activity to address any problems you see with them? (G)

ACTIVITY 2.4 ALL IN A PICTURE AND SNAPSHOT OF ME ACTIVITIES

Another activity that requires educators to think about and reveal particular aspects of their cultural identity is what we call a Snapshot of Me. For this project, participants choose one aspect of their identity to highlight that is particularly meaningful, but that others may not know about them because it is not a visible part of who they are as cultural beings. To share a Snapshot of Me, participants usually create a collage, a poster, or a slide show either on paper or electronically. However, prior to providing the directions for this activity, we conduct a related activity with the group that we call It's All in a Picture. For this activity, participants bring three to five pictures they have cut from magazines that they feel represent themselves in some way. Alternatively, we provide a large collection of pictures from magazines, perhaps 25 to 35 images depending on the size of the group. These pictures are placed on a large table or even on the floor, randomly mixed together and spread out. The next step is to ask everyone to come and pick out one picture, not one that they brought in themselves, that they feel represents some aspect of their identities. We then ask each person to explain why they selected what they did and how it represents some aspect of their identity. Most educators express their thinking in metaphors or similes, a form of synectics, which is a metaphorical process used for thinking and problem solving. We sometimes do this activity in small groups, asking grade-level teams or the math department faculty, for example, to select jointly one picture that represents them as cultural group. It can be challenging for some educators to make meaningful connections, but it is worthwhile if the goal is to extend thinking about the cultural subgroups they are a part of or for community building in a large group. We think this activity would be very useful for PLCs to do as well.

The All in a Picture activity is a bridge to the Snapshot of Me activity, where we ask each participant to create a collage, poster, or slide show either on paper or electronically to represent an aspect of their cultural identity. What some participants choose to reveal about themselves seem frivolous to others sometimes, but each individual has chosen to share something meaningful about aspects of their cultural identities. For example, we had an educator share "the culture of brides" because she was getting married soon, while others created posters about the culture of soccer or scrapbooking or gourmet cooking because these are important aspects of their identity. Still other educators create and share presentations about the culture of being a grandmother, about their Italian heritage, or their former life as a journalist. Others develop presentations about their culture as vegetarians, nonsmokers, or lesbians. The choice is completely up to the individual, and the guidelines are intentionally vague about how to represent one's cultural identity. We do, however, encourage the inclusion of many visuals in their Snapshot of Me presentations because we encourage conversations with others about the content. However, the same rules for respect and empathy apply, and it is crucial to create a climate of trust so that everyone feels safe and respected.

We also provide a personal example and show examples that others have created in previous workshops, using digital storytelling tools found on the Internet, such as VoiceThread, ScrapBlog, or TarHeel Reader or with Animoto, Prezi, or Vuvox. We suggest that educators consider using image-editing software such as Apple's iMovie, Microsoft's PhotoStory 3 or MovieMaker, Adobe's Premiere, and even PowerPoint for developing electronic presentations. However, we find that electronic versions of Snapshot of Me projects are used most often by high school students when teachers take this activity into their classrooms.

Objective

- To provide participants with an opportunity to represent and share an aspect of themselves as cultural beings
- To find common ground with others
- To build relationships between and among other educators

Instruction to Participant

Select one aspect of your cultural identity that you want others to know about you. Consider selecting something that others probably don't know about you, something that is a passion of yours or something that you want others to know about you.

Create a collage, a poster, or a slide show either on paper or electronically, including a variety of images to represent some aspect of your cultural identity. Be prepared to explain to others why you selected to share this particular snapshot of your cultural identity versus others you might have selected to share.

Recommended Questions Following the Snapshot of Me Activity (I=Individual Reflection Questions, G=Group Discussion Questions)

- What surprised you about other people's snapshots? (G)
- Did anything you learned about other people's cultural identities challenge or reinforce any stereotypes you have? Why or why not? (I, G)

(Continued)

(Continued)

- What can you learn about the concepts of identity and culture from this activity? (I, G)
- In what ways can sharing your snapshot engender connections or community building among your colleagues? (G)
- Is your snapshot appropriate to share with your students? With parents and families in your school? (I, G)
- What aspects of one's cultural identity are and are not appropriate to share publicly in your school and community? (G)

Time

- It takes two to three hours depending on how much research and detail educators choose to put into their creating presentations to convey a snapshot of me. The sharing or presentation of each person's Snapshot of Me project can take some time because conversations among the participants and debriefing afterward are very important. We usually do our sharing as a gallery walk. That is, a portion of the participants set up their posters, collages, or slide shows (running on laptops), and everyone else walks around to view each snapshot and talk with the creators. Another 20 to 30 minutes is devoted to the participants asking clarifying questions about individual snapshots and the facilitator asking reflection questions of the whole group. Time can also be made for several people to share their snapshots at the beginning of each session or all at one session, depending on the size of the group.

Revealing Beliefs and Identities to Others

Although many previous activities allow educators to express their individual or familial cultural identity in ways they want others to see them, other activities are more personal and private expressions of cultural identity that are important to us but that we may not want others to see. We find that exploring, reflecting on, unpacking, and sharing our identities in various ways helps educators become more culturally competent in their interactions with others. Some activities described later also provide quick but safe ways to continue on this path, such as participating in the Intercultural Autograph Hunt, described next, while other activities, such as the Bio-Poems and doing the Snapshot of Me presentation, require a little more thought. However, the final activity in this chapter, the Privilege Walk, explores issues more deeply and in ways that educators may not have thought about or revealed to others before. As a result, this activity feels riskier because it reveals layers that make up our individual cultural identities. In fact, each of the next three activities requires that educators progressively peel away the proverbial layers of the onion or to see parts of the iceberg below the water's surface, as they reveal aspects of their cultural identities that may not be obvious to others.

ACTIVITY 2.5 INTERCULTURAL AUTOGRAPH HUNT

We often use a version of a scavenger hunt that we call the Intercultural Autograph Hunt in an early session to uncover and celebrate the diversity within the group. This is certainly not a new activity, and it is often used as an icebreaker. We use it for that purpose, too, but we also use it to discover the assets we have in the group we are working with. We also use the results of what we learn about one another to discuss the complex nature of culture and the strengths educators bring to their work with diverse students. You can use the questions we provide in Resource 2.4 *Intercultural Autograph Hunt* located on the companion website for this book, or you can modify them to fit the group you are leading. Remember to have participants try to find a different person for each description, and remind them to talk with each person before asking for a signature.

Objective

- To provide participants with an opportunity to share various aspects of their cultural identities and to learn about the assets and strengths of others in the group

Instruction to Participants

Using Resource 2.4, talk to others to find out who can claim what they have accomplished, experienced, or have knowledge about using the statements in each box.

Have each person tell you a little bit about that topic, experience, or accomplishment and then ask for a signature in the appropriate box. Don't rush so much that you forget what you learned from talking with people—try to learn some new things and remember what you learned.

The goal is to get all the boxes signed by different people and to offer to sign for others if you have accomplished, experienced, or know something about the statements in any of the boxes.

(Continued)

(Continued)

Recommended Questions Following the Intercultural Autograph Hunt Activity (I=Individual Reflection Questions, G=Group Discussion Questions)

- After the participants have completed this activity, go through the list and ask for people who signed a particular item to raise their hands. Then ask the following questions:
  - ○ Which items are shared by the most people in the group? The fewest of people? (G)
  - ○ Which items were the most difficult to find an autograph for? The easiest? (G)
  - ○ What did you learn from your peers that you did not know or had not thought about before? (G)
  - ○ What are some other things we could have added to this Intercultural Autograph Hunt? (G)
  - ○ What do you think the purpose is of this activity? (I, G)
  - ○ How is this kind of information useful in establishing connections between people who are meeting for the first time? (I, G)
  - ○ How would this activity be similar or different if it is done in the classroom with students? (G)

Time

- Approximately 30 to 60 minutes depending on the size of the group and the number of items in the Intercultural Autograph Hunt

ACTIVITY 2.6 BIO-POEMS

Bio-Poems are a type of formula poetry that allows individuals to express "the me I want others to see" because they get to choose the ideas and words that they want to reveal to others about themselves, their interests, and their lives. Many teachers use Bio-Poems to help students express themselves and reveal their identity in writing. They also help teachers learn more about their students. The technique is simple, but effective, for eliciting a more nuanced answer to the question, Who Am I? We have provided both a template for creating a Bio-Poem and a sample Bio-Poem on the companion website for this book in Resource 2.5 *Format for Bio-Poem With Sample.*

Objective

- To provide participants with an opportunity to express what they want others to know about them

Instructions to Participants

Using the format in Resource 2.5, complete each of the 10 lines of this Bio-Poem by selecting what you want to share about yourself.

If you have time, you can decorate your Bio-Poem using the computer or other media. Be prepared to share your Bio-Poem with the group.

Recommended Questions Following the Bio-Poem Activity (I=Individual Reflection Questions, G=Group Discussion Questions)

- Who (or what) did you hear that you have in common with that person? (G)
- Was there a pattern or theme you hear when listening to everyone's Bio-Poems? (G)
- What was the hardest part about writing your Bio-Poem? Why? (I, G)
- What is the purpose of this activity in relation to diversity issues and critical cultural competence? (I, G)

Time

- It takes 30 to 40 minutes to complete the Bio-Poem, plus additional time to share Bio-Poems with the group and to debrief the process of creating the Bio-Poem.

ACTIVITY 2.7 THE PRIVILEGE WALK

One of our favorite activities over the years is based on Peggy McIntosh's classic article from 1990 titled "White Privilege: Unpacking the Invisible Knapsack." Even after 20 years, the observations made in this article about the hidden benefits of being White are still true for most White educators and still problematic for many people of color. The purpose of this identity-based activity is for educators to discover the diversity within themselves, as well as to experience how preconceived notions and beliefs about other people—friends, colleagues, and coworkers—affect

(Continued)

(Continued)

how they view others. This activity can be very emotional. Discussion of McIntosh's article and active engagement in the related Privilege Walk activity, described next, usually includes some denial, lots of thoughtful discussion, and many "aha" moments. Therefore, a substantial amount of time must be allotted for discussing, processing, and debriefing to ensure that no one leaves with misconceptions or reinforced stereotypes. Sensitivity on the part of the leader is also crucial in cases where some participants may become upset or choose not to participate.

The Privilege Walk activity has been used often in diversity workshops. It has also been modified depending on the time available. The goal is to help participants see and feel how certain identifiers associated with race, ethnicity, class, gender, ability, and religion are forms of privilege for some individuals and not for others. After establishing ground rules, participants stand in one line, side by side, without speaking to one another. Ground rules include establishing a safe and confidential learning environment because this activity asks people to reveal things about themselves that may not be visible or known to others. As the leader reads statements taken from searching the Internet for the "privilege walk" or uses those provided in Resource 2.6 *Statements for Privilege Walk Activity* on the companion website for this book, participants take one step forward or backward as directed or remain where they are if they feel a statement is not relevant to them or if they do not wish to respond. Debriefing after the activity is crucial, as it is with all the activities discussed in this book because this activity may stir up emotions.

Objective

- To provide participants with an opportunity to understand the intricacies of privilege

Instruction to Participants

Participants should stand shoulder to shoulder in a line across the room. Participants can release their hands, but they should be instructed to stand shoulder to shoulder in a straight line *without speaking*.

Instruct participants to listen carefully to each sentence, such as those listed in Resource 2.6, and to take the step required if the sentence applies to them. They may also be told there is a prize at the front of the site that everyone is competing for.

Recommended Questions Following the Privilege Walk Activity (I=Individual Reflection Questions, G=Group Discussion Questions)

Ask participants to remain in their positions and to look at their position relative to others and to also look at the positions of the other participants in their group. Ask participants to consider who among them would probably win the prize. Use these questions to debrief this activity:

- What happened? (I, G)
- How did this exercise make you feel? (I, G)
- What were your thoughts as you did this exercise? (I, G)
- What have you learned from this experience? (I, G)
- What can you do with this information in the future? (I, G)

Time

- It takes about one and one-half hours, although if fewer questions are asked, the time can be shortened.

Potential Challenges

When writing about their experiences following the Privilege Walk activity (Cooper, 2007), educators revealed a wide range of emotions, including feeling cathartic, nervous, marginalized, confused, isolated, distanced. They also wrote that it evoked bad memories. For example, three participants in the Privilege Walk activity wrote the following:

Consistently, I felt nervous and confused throughout the privilege activity. As many of my classmates began to move ahead of me, I felt isolated and distanced by their lack of shared experiences. At times, as I stepped further and further back, I felt guilty and wished to be in the middle (not the front, as guilt would also result from extreme privilege). Ultimately, I left sad and angry at the visual representation of my isolation and marginalization. Perhaps, I feel cheated that some part of me results in such a multitude of negative experiences.

This activity was hard for me to participate in. . . . I must admit that this activity made me ashamed, and I did not want others to know things about me. Even as I sit here now, I feel like others think differently about me. I feel like the way I have built up has crumbled, and I am not very comfortable with that.

The privilege activity made me feel upset and awkward. I was at the back of the group, and felt bad with everyone looking at me. . . . Also, answering those questions brought up a lot of bad memories for me. (Cooper, 2007, p. 250)

The Privilege Walk presents another noteworthy challenge: Some participants who move ahead attribute their location near or at the head the line to their parents' hard work. They are proud of the fact that their parents overcame adversity or sacrificed so they would have more advantages than their parents had. This pride causes some participants to be quite emotional, and this experience needs to be processed carefully. Such poignant stories may provoke discussion about the

(Continued)

(Continued)

myth of meritocracy. Some participants may remain oblivious or refuse to believe that hard work does not always reap benefits for all, especially those who have experienced various forms of oppression, prejudice, or discrimination. We cannot reiterate enough that deliberate, intentional discussions about the Privilege Walk, either preceded or followed by appropriate readings, are needed to debunk the myth of meritocracy and to generate dialogue about White privilege. It is also essential that the person who is leading the Privilege Walk activity and the follow-up discussion understands fully the implications of White privilege and is comfortable in guiding others to better understanding it as well.

   Although doing the Privilege Walk activity is uncomfortable and unsettling for some participants, even after our debriefing this activity or a similar one designed to reveal oneself to others, it remains vital for preparing educators for the community-based learning activities in Chapters 6 and 7.

SUMMARY OF KEY POINTS

This chapter provides a variety of strategies to help educators engage in critical self-reflection for identifying and sharing aspects of self and identity. We include many traditional activities commonly used to invite educators to explore and reveal their public and private identities. Some activities provide opportunities to share the "me I want others to see" and other activities reveal, perhaps, previously unrealized diversity. Such activities allow those participating to experience how preconceived notions and beliefs about other people, including friends, colleagues, and coworkers, affect how we view both ourselves and others. Individual reflection and group discussion questions are asked to elicit alternative perspectives and to make visible implicit personal biases or assumptions. We offer these activities to lay the foundation for understanding the importance of exploring the numerous individual and cultural assets that students, families, and the community bring to the classrooms, which are explored in later chapters.

REFLECTION AND EXTENSION

- Choose one of the All About Me activities described previously to do yourself, and use it to share aspects of your cultural identity that you want others to see.

- What are some other activities or reflection/discussion questions you know to use to help educators better understand themselves as cultural beings?
- How can you adopt some of your favorite activities so they work well in an online environment?

ADDITIONAL RESOURCES

- More activities for helping educators understand themselves as cultural beings and for answering the question of who they are as teachers and administrators can be found on Paul Gorski's Multicultural Pavilion section of the EdChange website at www.edchange.org/multicultural/activityarch.html.
- Additional All About Me activities for elementary students can be found on these websites:
  o www.alphabet-soup.net/me/me.html
  o www.enchantedlearning.com/themes/allaboutme.shtml

ONLINE EXTENSIONS

The Privilege Walk activity can also be done online through any synchronous conferencing or learning software, such as Elluminate or WebEx. To prepare for the activity online, a grid with lines indicating the space for participants to "step" back and forth needs to be created in PowerPoint or other applications compatible with the online learning tool being used. Participants need to be instructed to select an image to represent themselves online, or they can simply create a textbox and add their initials to participate in the activity. At the beginning of the activity, all participants will be instructed to align their images along the starting line and practice moving their images a step back (to a line below the starting line) or a step forward (to lines above the starting line) on the screen. When the facilitator reads or types in the statement from the Privilege Walk activity exactly as described earlier (see Resource 2.6), participants will move their image forward (toward the top of the screen) or back (toward the bottom of the screen) according to their answer. The facilitator may also choose to record the screen during the activity and replay the recording after the activity to invite discussion using the debriefing questions.

Nevertheless, the debriefing questions should follow immediately after this activity, preferably in some kind of synchronous format.

_____

_____

Starting Line

_____

_____

_____

FOCUS FOR PROFESSIONAL LEARNING COMMUNITIES (PLCs)

Many activities in this chapter, which are designed to learn and reveal more about the self, are suitable for PLCs, especially at the initial stages when the members are getting to know and trust one another. Teachers and administrators in PLCs often think they know their colleagues well, and many do, but in some cases, important beliefs, values, and cultural identities that will impact the work of the PLC may not have been revealed previously. For this reason, we recommend that members of PLCs, who value becoming critically culturally competent, use the questions posed for developing an autobiography (see Activity 2.1 and Resource 2.2) or teaching philosophy (see Activity 2.2 and Resource 2.3). The All About Me activities, the Snapshot of Me activity, the Intercultural Autograph Hunt, and Bio-Poems might also be tried with students in the elementary and middle grades and the results shared in PLCs. However, we recommend asking an experienced facilitator to conduct and debrief the Privilege Walk activity, if this is the choice for a PLC.

Resource 2.1 Suggestions for Leading and Participating in Democratic Discussions

Resource 2.2 Alternative Autobiographical Sketch

Resource 2.3 Questions to Help You Develop Your Educational Philosophy

Resource 2.4 Intercultural Autograph Hunt

Resource 2.5 Format for Bio-Poem With Sample

Resource 2.6 Statements for Privilege Walk Activity

3

Moving From Beliefs and Visions to Action

How Can We Link Our Personal and Professional Identities?

Introduction

Developing critical cultural competence in educators requires a deep and nuanced understanding of themselves as cultural beings and explicit awareness of how their personal and professional lives are linked. The activities in this chapter are provided to help educators become aware of how their beliefs, goals, and visions are reflected in judgments they make and actions they take, which, in turn, influence the learning opportunities they offer their K–12 students. We also describe how educators can undertake action research projects to help them enact their visions and beliefs in their classrooms and schools. Therefore, this chapter focuses on three processes that link to the goal of further developing educators with critical cultural competence. They include the following:

- Developing a vision for what kind of educator you want to be and how to impact your students' live

- Engaging in personal theorizing that leads to uncovering your personal practical theories (PPTs), which are your pedagogical beliefs that guide your practice
- Undertaking action research to improve your practice to benefit your students

While we have extensive experience working with educators on each of these processes in different contexts, we describe visioning, PPTs, and action research in this chapter specifically for the professional development environment. However, none of these processes can be completed in one session, so they are best suited for long-term professional development. Therefore, described later are steps that can be carried out over time in a more in-depth, extended format for professional development that occurs throughout a school year, or perhaps, it is started in a summer workshop and continued into the school year. Also, engaging in visioning, making one's PPTs explicit, and doing action research are excellent activities for members of professional learning communities (PLCs) to undertake as a part of their ongoing work toward increasing student achievement. In all cases, the goal for the activities described is to move from thoughts to actions and to move educators toward critical cultural competence by meeting the needs of their diverse learners.

ACTIVITY 3.1 VISIONING

Visioning in an educational (as opposed to an organizational or corporate) context is a conscious process of reflecting on your sense of self as an educator, your beliefs, your work, your images and metaphors around education, and your personal goals for how all these might play out in your practice. The product of such reflection is a statement about what kind of educator you want to be, what you want your students to be like and/or to learn because of being in your class or your school, and how your values and ideals would look in actual practice. Though rooted in reflection on your prior beliefs and personal theories about students, teaching, learning, leadership, and the curriculum, your vision describes a personal commitment to inspire students in ways that tend to be more morally than cognitively based (Fairbanks et al., 2010).

Educational scholars have defined visioning in several ways. For example, Duffy (2002) sees visioning from a moral position, asserting that educators' ultimate goals and responsibilities are what their students will become as adults. Hammerness (2003) sees visioning from a more intellectual perspective, as helping teachers develop a clearer sense of their purposes for teaching. She thinks of a vision as the teacher's "images of ideal classroom practice" (Hammerness, 2006, p. 1). Shulman and Shulman (2004) and Kennedy (2006) similarly define visions as images of particular learning activities that represent what a teacher envisions before teaching a lesson. Sometimes vision focuses on students, especially on what kind of people educators want their students to become under their guidance. Sometimes vision focuses on how educators seek either a moral and/or intellectual outcome for their vision, which then guides their interactions with students (Rattigan-Rohr, 2005). Nevertheless, all visions express educators' personal self-understandings about their commitment to extended outcomes (Fairbanks et al., 2010). For example, one teacher's vision may be about helping her students make good choices and become good problem solvers, while another educator may have a vision for his students become good citizens who are able to work well with others in a community. Still another educator may enact her vision as in this example from a first-grade teacher:

> Her vision—that is, her deeper reason for teaching—was for her students to embrace a sense of fair play and equity in their interpersonal lives. When beginning a guided reading lesson, her goal was simply to develop reading skills. But when her students looked at the pictures of the main character and said it was a boy because the character had short hair and was dressed in jeans, the teacher saw an opportunity to develop her vision for teaching. She had them read the first page, where (as she knew they would) they discovered that the main character's name was Jennifer. At this point, the teacher spontaneously inserted a mini-lesson on the danger of stereotyping, offering varying examples until the students demonstrated understanding of her goals and objectives. She could have settled for routine implementation of guided reading. But her vision for how she wanted to touch the future through her students drove her to look for opportunities that went beyond standard reading goals and objectives. (Fairbanks et al, 2010, p. 164)

We believe that visioning is a crucial process for educators to undertake to develop critical cultural competence because visions serve as a moral or cognitive compass with which they can adjust their practices. In fact, Shulman (2004) suggested that visioning may be the "missing construct" in identifying high-quality teachers, and Hammerness and her colleagues, in Darling-Hammond and Bransford (2005), see visioning as a vital process in helping teachers develop their professional identity.

Although there are different ways to elicit visions (cf. Hammerness, 2006), we (and the educators we work with) have found great value in the following a four-step process for developing a vision. Educators can achieve a deeper awareness of what motivates them as educators, (re)discover their reasons for becoming a teacher or administrator, and (re)claim their strengths by dreaming about how they want to be remembered, designing a metaphor to describe themselves as an educator, and explaining how they can take action to deliver their vision.

(Continued)

(Continued)

Objective

- To provide participants with the opportunity to articulate their vision for themselves and their students

Instruction to Participants

Use following questions to help you develop your vision for who/how you want to be as a teacher or administrator, and what/how you want your students to be like after being in your classroom or your school for a year.

Discover. Reflecting on your personal values and prior learning experiences (including both school experiences and nonschool experiences), why did you choose to become an educator? What personal strengths prepare you to be a good teacher or administrator? Describe the values, skills, strengths, and qualities you bring to your classroom or school.

Dream. Imagine 20 years from now, when the students you worked with come back to visit you. What would they say to you? What would you say when you are interviewed as a recipient of the Excellence Award for Educators? What does a person with your values, skills, strengths, and qualities want to accomplish next? What do you hope and dream to achieve? What would be the ideal teaching and learning environment for you?

Design. What will you do to achieve your dream? Which of your strengths, skills, and qualities will you use to attain your vision? Compose a metaphor that captures what being an educator is for you.

Deliver. What knowledge or experiences do you think you need to achieve your dream? What actions do you plan to take to become an excellent teacher or administrator? What are the first steps? What might be your obstacles? What would you do if you face those challenges?

We usually revisit the initial vision statements that educators develop at the end of our time with them and ask them to revise their visions based on what they have learned in our diversity workshops. As a result, we—and they—often see a shift in their visions that shows growth in becoming more critically culturally competent. Here are some examples of parts of vision statements written by teachers we have worked with:

Jessica's Vision

Over the years, I have learned that in this society we are putting our children in a box. By the third grade, our students are no longer individuals full of potential, but statistics and scores on an end of grade test. I have a big problem with this picture. I decided that I was so passionate about this issue that I needed to be in the system to promote change. I am not in the field of education to simply continue the learning cycle that we are on, but to challenge it to meet the needs of all students. I want to help be the catalyst for change our education system so desperately needs.

Because of the type of vision I have, I don't expect to see the kind of results I want right away. My success is not based on assessment scores or even popularity with the students. My success will be measured by the lives of my students, years after they have left my classroom. I want to set the solid base from which a life of unlimited potential can grow. If a past student of mine walks up to me one day and says, "You made me believe in myself," I will know that I have done my job. I had some powerful teachers in my past that have given me the skills and faith that I can reach my dreams, and I want to do the same for my future students. I want to give my students options and the courage to know that they can do any of them if that is what they desire. When all is said and done, I want to look back at my life and know that I made a positive impact on the world. . . .

My ultimate dream is to make this world a better place. It seems quite lofty and unattainable when you look at it directly. The key to attaining my goals is to break things down into manageable pieces. . . . This is how I want to accomplish my dreams as a teacher. I want to reach one child at time. If I can make a positive difference in one child, then I have made a difference in every person in that child's life.

Jane's Vision

I work with students because I want to be a positive force in their lives and to help guide them in a productive and fulfilling path in life. I hope that many of my students take my advice and go to college, which in a school district with a very high dropout rate would be a great achievement. I truly hope to infect them with a love of learning, regardless of the subject matter that they are learning about. Last, I think that as long as they tell me that I had some impact on their lives, then I will feel that I was a successful teacher. After all, teaching, to me, is inspiring a future generation to pass on the passion of lifelong learning.

I have always felt very strongly about treating students fairly and giving them opportunity to develop regardless of ethnicity, gender, the like, but a but in looking into classrooms at my school, that belief only grew further

(Continued)

(Continued)

into my drive to change the wrongs that I feel are being done, particularly to our English Learners (ELs).

Next semester, I want to continue to develop my Tolerance Club plans and continue to encourage my students and faculty members to do more to engage in discussions to provide a school community where everyone is included and treated fairly. I truly hope that I can be a factor in motivating change in the lives and beliefs of people around me. I also want to continue to read and develop more knowledge about my subject matter, and plan to incorporate that into my classroom in the fall.

To achieve my dreams, I need the cooperation of my administration and to possibly get a grant from Tolerance.org to obtain more materials for my classroom and club. Also, I need to get my students to participate and spread these ideals further into their communities and classes. I also need to get other teachers involved to help encourage other teachers to change their ways and start different approaches to students that they may have discriminated against or ignored in the past. I know that this task will take a lot of passion and determination, which are strengths I feel I will draw from to make this possible. . . . The idea that one person can make a difference has always been a strong belief of mine, and I hope to create a chain reaction that will continue to influence these students and their community even after I have them in class or in my club.

Recommended Discussion Questions Following the Activity (I=Individual Reflection Questions, G=Group Discussion Questions)

- What kinds of new knowledge or experiences have influenced your vision? (I)
- How has your vision changed over time? Why do you think it has changed? (I, G)
- What kinds of things do you find yourself doing in your classroom or in your school that are guided by your vision? (I, G)

Time

- It takes one to three hours of reflection and writing time to develop a vision statement, plus additional time to share and discuss the visioning process in either small or large groups.

As mentioned previously, other ways to elicit visions include one process that Hammerness (2006) tried with more than 80 high school teachers in her research on visioning. Hammerness recommends placing each of the questions found in Resource 3.1, located on the companion website for this book, at the top of a new piece of paper so teachers have plenty of space to write their responses.

ACTIVITY 3.2 PERSONAL PRACTICAL THEORIES (PPTs)

PPTs are the pedagogical beliefs educators hold that guide their practices regarding teaching, learning, curriculum, students, schooling, leadership, and the like. By engaging in a process known as personal theorizing, educators can explicitly describe their PPTs (Chant, Heafner, & Bennett, 2004; He & Levin, 2008; Levin & He, 2008). Different from vision statements, PPTs usually tend to be beliefs about pedagogy, rather than about an educator's moral, ethical, or religious beliefs, for example.

Research about teacher beliefs indicates that their pedagogical beliefs influence their actions in the classroom (Chant, 2009; Chant et al., 2004; Pajares, 1992; Richardson, 1996, 2003) and, therefore, the opportunities their students have to learn. Some researchers have found that teachers' beliefs are resistant to change even with interventions (Wideen, Mayer-Smith, & Moon, 1998), while others have reported that teachers' beliefs continue to develop and change as they gain more teaching experience (Chant, 2009; Chant et al., 2004; Fives & Buehl, 2008) and that teachers expect such change regarding their understanding of teaching (Buehl & Fives, 2009). In our research, we have found that PPTs serve as goals for teachers and that PPTs usually have to do with pedagogical practices, which if enacted successfully will help educators' achieve their vision (Levin, He, & Allen, 2010). Also, we have found that for professional development to stick, and for teachers to make real changes in their practices as a result, we need to know explicitly what their beliefs are. We also need to address beliefs directly in our professional development work and connect the participants' current beliefs to what we are trying to accomplish—and we need to do this openly. If we do not know where educators are coming from and what they believe—in this case regarding their beliefs about themselves as cultural beings, their beliefs about student diversity, and their beliefs about their students' families and home communities—then we can miss the mark, miss connecting with them, and, ultimately, find no change in their practice (or their beliefs) because of our professional development.

Examples of PPTs

To better understand what PPTs are, here are several examples from teachers we have worked with to show what each values and emphasizes in their teaching. Resource 3.2 *The Personal Theorizing Process*, located on the companion website for this book, is a PowerPoint presentation. We use it to share more examples of PPTs and to discuss if these educators might be elementary, middle, or high school teachers based on how they convey their PPTs.

(Continued)

(Continued)

Margaret's PPTs

1. All children are unique and individual
2. High expectations for all children (personal best, which is different for every child)
3. Positive atmosphere
4. Bring children's different cultures to the classroom

Carolyn's PPTs

1. Treat all students fairly but not the same
2. Believe that all students can learn to their individual potential
3. Embracing all differences
4. Differentiate
5. Students are teachers too

Jennifer's PPTs

1. Model the social and academic skills that they want to teach their students
2. Have a successful learning environment; the classroom must feel and be like a community.
3. Know my students to understand their individual strengths, needs, and backgrounds
4. Take risks and be able to make mistakes
5. Know the families of the children I teach
6. Incorporate technology
7. Civic and social development

By using all three steps in the personal theorizing process described later, you can help teachers and administrators make their PPTs explicit so they are clearly articulated and, therefore, available for examination. Engaging in this process helps educators develop a deeper understanding of themselves and develop more awareness about how their personal and professional lives are linked in their work with students, families, and communities. This process assists educators in developing critical cultural competence because they become explicitly aware of their beliefs and how congruent their beliefs are with their actions.

Step 1. Ask educators to brainstorm, write about, and share their PPTs.

Step 2. Have educators gather data to determine if they are actually carrying out and enacting their PPTs in their practice.

Step 3. Ask educators to create an action plan for enacting one of their PPTs that they have not been doing in their practice, for whatever reason, or that they really want to get better at by focusing on it.

Instructions for these three steps in the personal theorizing process are described in more detail next.

We recommend beginning with the first step, which is the least time intensive, as a part of any professional development. However, for professional development that is focused on helping educators actually change their practice, we highly recommend completing all three steps.

Objective

- To provide participants with the opportunity to make the content and sources of their usually implicit pedagogical beliefs explicit
- To gather and examine evidence of whether participants are enacting their PPTs in their practice
- To create an action plan to work toward enacting (or better enacting) one PPT

Instruction to Participants for Step 1: Making Your PPTs Explicit

Think and then write your answer to this essential question, *What are your beliefs and personal theories about teaching, learning, children, curriculum, leadership, and schooling?* Reflect on what you think are four to seven beliefs or personal practical theories that guide your work with students/teachers. Try to state them as clearly as possible at this time.

Define, elaborate on, and justify each one of your PPTs considering the following questions.

- What exactly do you mean by each PPT? Explain each one clearly.
- What are examples of how your PPTs look in the classroom/school?
- Where are the sources of each of your PPTs?
- Is there an order to your PPTs, or are they equally important? Reflect on this and explain your thinking.

Note: Be sure to write in first person to explain what you personally believe, not what you think other educators *should* believe. Also note that sources of PPTs can include one or more of the following possibilities: family values, cultural beliefs, your experience as a K–12 student, your teacher or administrator preparation program (including courses, theories, professors, or readings), experiences as a novice teacher or administrator, other educators you have observed, books or other readings, your recent experiences as an educator, professional development, and the like.

(Continued)

(Continued)

We also recommend that educators create a one-page graphic image or graphic organizer to display the connections among their PPTs. This image can then be shared easily with others in professional development sessions who probably will not read the full description of one another's PPTs. However, writing about one's PPTs should precede creation of the graphic so educators have the opportunity to reflect deeply on the beliefs that guide their practice. Furthermore, we encourage the use of technology to create the one-page graphic or graphic organizer, although it may also be draw by hand. The point is to symbolize one's pedagogical beliefs about teaching, learning, students, curriculum, leadership, and schooling, and the like in some kind of alternative representation, and doing so graphically requires a different type of thinking. This example is just one way to display PPTs graphically, but Resource 3.3 *Example of PPT Graphics: The Sky Is the Limit* and Resource 3.4 *Example of PPT Graphics: Unearthing Planet PPT*, found on the companion website for this book, show additional examples of PPT graphics that show the range of possibilities.

Recommended Discussion Questions Following the Activity (I=Individual Reflection Questions, G=Group Discussion Questions)

When it is time to share and process their PPTs, we ask educators to discuss the following questions, usually with a partner or in a small group:

- How are your PPTs similar or different compared to others in your group? (G)
- What are the benefits to you as an educator in articulating your PPTs? (I, G)
- Which of your PPTs relates to diverse students and/or working with their families and communities? (I, G)
- How does the process of surfacing your PPTs help you better understand yourself as a professional educator? (I, G)

Time

- It takes about two to three hours for brainstorming and writing for Step 1, making your PPTs explicit, although we always recommend that this time be broken into smaller segments rather than completed in one sitting, and another hour or so to create a graphic or graphic organizer to represent the connections among PPTs.

Instruction to Participants for Step 2: Evaluating Your PPTs in Action

The goal for this step of the personal theorizing process for educators is to gather evidence to determine whether their PPTs are actually present in the planning (preactive) phase for teaching and/or in the classroom interaction and teaching (interactive) phase and/or in the reflection (postactive) phase of teaching. For administrators, evidence from these three phases—preactive/planning, interactive/actions, and postactive/reflection—can also guide data collection. To see if your PPTs are being enacted in your practice, evidence for a particular PPT should be triangulated from three different data sources (e.g., a mentor's observation, student survey results, and weekly plans), or from the same type of data at three different times (e.g., three observations over time). What follows are directions for gathering evidence of PPTs in action, and for analyzing and writing about this evidence to show whether PPTs are actually being enacted in practice:

1. Gather data from a minimum of three (3) different sources (or from the same source three times) to assess at least four of your PPTs selected from those in Step 1.

2. Suggested sources of evidence to collect and analyze include, but are not limited to, the following:

   a. Administrator observation(s)

   b. Mentor observation(s)

   c. Peer observation(s)

   d. Audio and video recording of lesson(s)

   e. Reflective writings (e.g., National Board portfolios, responses to formal observations by administrators, department heads, or mentors)

   f. Your evaluation of artifacts (lesson plans, student work samples, tests, comments on student papers, bulletin boards, newsletters, other documents and communications, etc.)

   g. Student or teacher surveys or interviews

3. Review each piece of evidence to see what it tells you about how well you actually carry out your PPTs in practice.

4. For each of the four PPTs, describe the data you collected for each PPT along with an evaluative statement about whether you think it provides good evidence that you are carrying out that PPT.

5. Alternatively, you can create a table to include the different sources of data you collected as evidence for the four PPTs, and include your evaluation in each box.

Use Resource 3.5 *Format of Evaluation of Your PPTs in Action,* provided on the website companion for this book, to format Step 2, evaluating your PPTs in action.

Also see Resource 3.6 *Sample Analysis of PPTs in Action* for partial example of how a completed analysis of your PPTs might look when formatted in a table.

(Continued)

(Continued)

Recommended Questions Following the Activity (I=Individual Reflection Questions, G=Group Discussion Questions)

These questions can be discussed with a partner or in small groups, or they can also be used as written reflection questions.

- How well do you, *or* do you not, enact each of your PPTs in practice? (I)
- On further reflection, would you consider adding, dropping, or modifying any of your PPTs? Why or why not? If you decide to add to or revise one of your PPTs, how would it read? (I, G)
- What were the benefits and the difficulties in evaluating your PPTs? (I, G)
- Which of your PPTs do you think you would like to learn more about and/ or undertake an action research project to help you achieve it or enact it more systematically in your class? (I)

Time

- The process of data gathering, analyzing the evidence found, and either creating a chart like the examples in Resources 3.5 and 3.6 or writing about the evidence you have to show that you are enacting your PPTs will take several hours, perhaps three to four.

Instruction to Participants for Step 3:
Using Your PPTs to Plan an Action Research Project

Step 3 in the personal theorizing process involves educators choosing one PPT as the basis for planning an action research. It should be something a teacher or administrator would like to know more about, do more with in the classroom or school, or enact more systematically. Because Step 3 of the personal theorizing process partially overlaps with action research described in Activity 3.3 Action Research, we describe this process next. The main difference between Step 3 of the personal theorizing process, which is only the planning phase of an action research project based on one PPT, and Activity 3.3 is that we describe the entire process of conducting an action research next.

ACTIVITY 3.3 ACTION RESEARCH

Action research has been defined as "systematic, intentional inquiry by teachers" (Lytle & Cochran-Smith, 1990, p.83). Also, it is described as research that educators do to investigate their professional practice, to understand and improve the nature and specifics of their work, and to develop a stronger voice when communicating about it (Oberg & McCutcheon, 1987). Kemmis and McTaggart (1988) said that action research requires teachers to engage in a cycle of questioning, planning, reflecting, acting, observing, reflecting, replanning, and often questioning further. This process sets critical, reflective action research apart from ordinary problem solving that educators do every day. Therefore, action research is an excellent professional development experience for challenging educators to examine their practice critically and systematically.

The purpose of action research, as the name conveys literally, is about taking action based on research. Action research engages educators in conducting research in their classroom or school to improve student learning, to solve practical problems, to gather a deeper understanding of students, or to examine their practices systematically and critically. During this process, educators develop as reflective practitioners because they have to think about not only what they are going to do but also how and why. The goal of action research is to make changes or find ways to modify things that are not working.

Action research can be conducted by teachers in their classrooms to improve their practice, by teams of teachers working in pairs or small groups on a common problem of interest to all, or by larger groups at a grade level or department or even schoolwide, and by administrators individually or in collaboration with other educators. PLCs are ideal groups for undertaking action research. Depending on the focus of action research, the cyclical process of questioning, planning, reflecting, acting, observing, reflecting, replanning, and questioning has the potential to help educators develop critical cultural competence.

Differences between action research and traditional educational research are highlighted in Figure 3.1, so the practical and personal nature of action research is

Figure 3.1 Comparing Traditional Educational Research to Action Research

Traditional Educational Research	Action Research
Problem based on an implication or interpretation of a theory	Problem or question arises from a desire to improve practice
Purpose is to support hypotheses that apply across the population	Purpose is to construct knowledge about self and situation and to take practice in new directions
Proposed actions are based on reflection of theory	Proposed actions are based on reflection of one's perceptions
Focus of the research is on educational theory	Focus of the research is on practice and theory, which are seen as a single concept
Colleagues are used as a source of theory and as critics of work	Colleagues are used as collaborators and mutual reflectors
Relationship with students is as observer to subjects	Relationship with students is learner to learner
Successful research brings changes in universal understanding	Successful research brings understanding of self and situation

(Continued)

(Continued)

compared to the more theoretical and decontextualized nature of how most educators understand traditional research. Action research can arise from classroom or schoolwide concerns; a desire to help students or to improve one's practice; or to understand teaching, learning, the curriculum, and students in new ways. Action research is not something done to teachers and administrators by outsiders, but rather, it is something they undertake themselves as insiders to take action, to achieve a goal, to enact one of their PPTs more systematically, or to try something that might help students at the individual classroom level or even schoolwide.

Objective

- To provide participants with a systematic way to implement or change something to improve their practice and/or help their students

Instruction to Participants

The following basic steps for doing action research can be used to lead educators through the action research process.

- Identify your interests, curiosities, problems, goals, or topics you may want to explore or change.
- Read and research to learn more about your research interest(s).
- Develop and refine your research question(s).
- Develop a plan of action for what, when, where, and how you can answer your research question(s).
- Collect several different kinds of data.
- Analyze your data.
- Take action and share your results with others.
- Consider additional questions and future research.

Action research projects can begin with educators planning ways to achieve their vision or enact one of their PPTs. Action research can also start with a wish to understand something better or with a dissatisfaction, a nagging concern, a desire to change or to refine something, a student whose needs are not being met, a challenge, a problem, or a chronic issue. Teacher researchers may consider focusing on one student, studying a small group of students, revamping one area of the curriculum, doing something to fix a chronic problem in the classroom, trying something new, studying the social issues in the classroom, or working with other educators.

Once an interest, curiosity, problem, goal, or topic has been identified, the next step is to develop preliminary research question(s) to focus on. Many action researchers begin by asking, *how, what,* or *what if?* For example, if the PPT I really want to enact has to do with building a stronger sense of community in my classroom, then I might ask, "How can I use morning meetings to build a sense of community in my classroom?" or "What happens when I use cooperative group learning activities more often in my class?" or "Would using both of these practices more systematically help develop a stronger sense of community in our classroom?" Or if my vision is for my students to understand what equity and social justice mean in the real world, I could ask, "What do the students in my school need to read or experience to help them to better understand equity and social justice?" or "What if we engage in service learning projects in our community to help others less fortunate than we are?" or "How could we create a website or wiki to show the ways we understand equity and social justice?"

Action research questions that are not worth asking include those with yes-or-no answers, questions that educators can figure out easily by reading the literature about their topic of interest, or questions that they already know the answer to and just want to prove something. Good action research questions, however, are not easy to develop, and can take on many forms, as Hubbard and Power (2003) indicate in their book about action research, *The Art of Classroom Inquiry*. In their first chapter, Hubbard and Power suggest encouraging teachers to transform their wonderings into research questions. We reproduced a list of possible action research questions taken from Hubbard and Power as examples to help educators think about their questions in Resource 3.7 *Action Research Questions (Hubbard & Power, 2003)*, located on the companion website for this book.

The next step is to learn what others have done that is relevant to your action research topic. The process of doing background research is useful in getting ideas about what teachers or administrators might try and study in their classrooms or schools, but it also helps in finding ways to study the topic of interest. Consulting what others have written also helps educators refine their initial research questions. Doing background research can be accomplished before or after reflecting on particular interests, curiosities, problems, goals, or topics. Both teachers and administrators may want to learn what others have found to be successful *before* starting their action research projects, or they may want to compare what they found because of their action research with others *after* they have analyzed their data. In other words, going to the research literature to learn what others have done can be useful at several points in the action research cycle.

As part of the planning process, educators also need to decide how they are going to gather evidence to answer their research question(s), what kind of data they might collect, how they can gather data systematically, and what kind of time frame should be used. This is what sets action research apart from what educators do every day because teachers and administrators are always trying new things and trying to fix chronic problems. Action researchers must be careful to systematically study what they are doing, collect evidence over time, and analyze it to look for patterns, themes, or numeric differences. Also, doing action researcher requires consideration about how to balance the roles of researcher and teacher or

(Continued)

(Continued)

researcher and administrator so they can continue to do their regular job well while gathering data. Such a balancing act requires planning, and selecting authentic data. Some of the following kinds of evidence can be collected for action research projects, depending on their appropriateness for answering the research question(s):

- Student work samples, including portfolios of work
- Assessments—results of tests, quizzes, and the like
- Scores on assignment rubrics
- Checklists of skills, behaviors, resources, and the like
- Other artifacts such as lesson plans, unit plans, or comments on student papers
- Student/parent surveys or interviews
- Observation/reflection journal or field notes
- Audio and/or video recording
- Administrator, mentor, or peer observations

Of course, once educators have collected data over time, usually for at least four to six weeks, they will need to analyze their data. This usually starts by organizing all the data that has been collected, reading through everything multiple times, and making notes. The goal of the analysis is to look for patterns or themes that are repeated in the data, to make comparisons between evidence collected at the beginning and at the end of their action research study, and then to code or otherwise locate and highlight evidence that answers the research question(s). Often, it helps to create charts and graphs to display the data collected, and it is very important to make note of (and share) unique or surprising findings as well.

When it is time to write the findings, we suggest that educators report the results of their action research project chronologically, by discussing each of the data sources collected one at a time or by discussing each of the patterns of themes detected in the data. If there is more than one research question, answering each one in turn is an effective way to report the findings. Writing an action research report is simply telling the story of what was undertaken, how it was accomplished, and what was learned as a result. Supporting evidence in the form of scores or frequency counts, and especially in the form of powerful quotes, anecdotes based on observations, or comments or descriptions of student and/or teacher behaviors will make the story real because the next step, after taking action(s) and making changes based on the results, is to share what was learned with others.

Disseminating the results of action research projects is a crucial step. This can be done formally or informally, but it needs to happen. Educators can present their results to relevant groups including grade-level teams, PLCs, and other action researchers; the school's administration and/or parent group; and, certainly, the students who participated with them in the action research process. Presentations can be formal or informal, but in most cases, presenting the results using visuals (graphs, charts, photos, video, maps, etc.) will help convey the results more clearly. Technology can be a useful tool in analyzing, reporting, and presenting the results of action research.

When educators analyze their data, reflect on what it means, and prepare to share it with others, they usually find that they have more questions, new curiosities, nagging concerns, and additional problems that are worthy of further action research. This is why the action research process is very cyclical with the results of one action research project leading to more questions, to more research, and to more data collection and analysis. In fact, this is normal, so suggesting future action research questions should be a part of reflecting on and writing about action research projects. For example, either during or after the time spent sharing the results of action research projects, we often ask the following questions:

Recommended Questions Following the Activity (I=Individual Reflection Questions, G=Group Discussion Questions)

- What new interests, curiosities, problems, goals, or topics have been raised for you because of conducting this action research project? (I, G)
- If you were to study this same question, or a new question, what would you do differently? What would you keep that worked well for you? (I)
- What was your most effective source of data or data-collection procedure? (I, G)
- What was the most challenging part of completing your action research project? Why do you think it was so challenging? (I, G)
- What did you learn about yourself as an educator while doing action research? As a researcher? As a reflective practitioner? (I)
- What did you learn that helped you develop critical cultural competence? (I, G)

Time

- Action research takes a great deal of time and needs to be spread over, at least, a semester, if not an entire school year, to be meaningful. We often plan action research projects during summer institutes or workshops or take the first three to four months at the beginning of a school year for planning action research. We then collect data for about four to eight weeks, followed by allowing another month for data analysis.

This is why action research is especially suited for those engaged in PLCs, and is not suitable at all for short-term professional development. Using Resource 3.8 *Guidelines for Action Research*, provided on the companion website for this book, is useful for keeping educators focused and on track as they complete their action research plans.

(Continued)

(Continued)

Examples of Action Research

Links to websites with two excellent examples of action research highlight the kinds of questions asked by educators who display critical cultural competence in the curiosities that drove the development of their action research projects. In these two examples, one a primary-grade teacher in Chicago and pair of high school teachers in New York City, all members of the Teachers Network Learning Institute (TNLI), have shared their action research projects. "TNLI was established to improve student achievement by bringing the teachers voice to education policymaking. Through action research, TNLI teachers seek to bring their experience and expertise to current debates on education policy" (Fenton, 1996, para. 2). In addition to these examples, we strongly recommend looking at many other resources available on the Teachers Network website: www.teachersnetwork.org/tnli/.

- Liz Goss's research titled "Learning to be a Good Guy: Teaching Social Justice in the Primary Classroom" at www.teachersnetwork.org/tnli/research/achieve/goss.htm.
- Jeremy Copeland and Jen Dyer's research titled "Lumps in the Melting Pot: What Happens When Diversity Isn't Enough" at www.teachersnetwork.org/tnli/research/change/copelanddryer.htm

SUMMARY OF KEY POINTS

In this chapter, we described three activities or processes that we believe are crucial steps in developing critical cultural competence:

- Developing a vision
- Using the personal theorizing process to identify one's PPTs
- Conducting action research

Engagement in each of these activities requires educators to consciously identify and then act on their vision for what kind of teacher or administrator they want to be or what kind of people they want their students to become, and then identify and enact their pedagogical beliefs, or PPTs, that guide their actions. The first two processes are highly reflective, as is the process of undertaking action research projects, which may be based on educators seeking to enact their visions and beliefs. Directions for how to elicit educators' visions and PPTs are included, along with a full explanation of the steps needed to complete action research projects. Examples of vision statements,

PPTs, and action research projects conducted by educators with critical cultural competence are also provided.

REFLECTION AND EXTENSION

- What is your vision for what you want educators to be like after having engaged in professional development around issues of equity, diversity, and critical cultural competence?
- What are your personal beliefs about how you can best engage educators in developing critical cultural competence?
- What questions do you think would be worth exploring in action research projects related to equity, diversity, and critical cultural competence?

ADDITIONAL RESOURCES

In Resource 3.9 *Additional Resources to Support Action Research*, located on the companion website for this book, we recommend several books about action research and list several websites from around the globe that offer excellent resources regarding action research.

ONLINE EXTENSIONS

Matt Wayne, New York City teacher, teacher researcher, and member of the Teachers Network (www.teachersnetwork.org/) involves his middle school students in an action research project that helps them learn about their book discussion habits by using a fishbowl technique. Here is a website to an explanation of Matt's action research project via streaming video showing how to do action research *with* students: www.teachersnetwork.org/teachnetnyc/mattwayne/action res.htm.

If you have Window Media Player on your computer, take a look at nine videos that provide explanations of action research (Introduction to Action Research, Preparation, Create the Plan, Act the Plan, and Share) on the website sponsored by *The Northeast Florida Science, Technology, and Mathematics Center for Education*. Interviews of teachers engaged in doing action research can also be found on this same website: www.nefstem.org/teacher_guide/materials/videos .htm.

You can read this online booklet, titled *How to Do Action Research in Your Classroom*: *Lesson Learned From the Teacher Network Leadership Institute*, written by Frances Rust and Christopher Clark at www.teachersnetwork.org/tnli/Action_Research_Booklet.pdf. The ideas described in this booklet for gathering data for action research projects are all excellent.

FOCUS FOR PROFESSIONAL LEARNING COMMUNITIES (PLCs)

As mentioned earlier, each of the three activities described in this chapter (visioning, PPTs, and action research) are all excellent processes for members of PLCs to engage in. Not only do they require extended periods to do well, they can make the joint work of the PLC more successful because the visions, beliefs, and values of individual members have been shared and honored. The process of identifying and sharing one's vision can be done by individual teachers and administrators in a PLC, but this process can also be undertaken to identify a joint vision for the PLC. Surfacing and making one's PPTs explicit is important to the success of PLCs because teachers' beliefs (and visions) serve as filters for how well they will engage in, understand, and actually carry out the work of the PLC. Finally, action research can and should be embedded into the work of PLCs. Members can carry out both individual and collaborative action research projects related to the goals of the PLC. In fact, we believe that there probably is no better way to assess the success of the work of PLCs than to carry out action research.

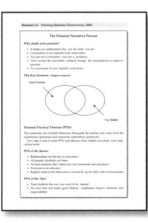

4

How Do We Prepare Educators to Understand and Appreciate Student Diversity?

Introduction

Reflecting on our assumptions, biases, beliefs, and visions for teaching prepares all educators to have an open mind for learning about and from our students with diverse backgrounds. Even though most educators recognize the importance of learning about the characteristics of diverse learners, very few have developed systematic ways to do so. No doubt, fewer apply what they learn from their interactions with their students to transform their teaching and to promote equity in education. In Chapters 4 and 5, we discuss goals and approaches for developing teachers and administrators' critical cultural competence through their interactions with diverse student populations. In Chapter 4, we focus on ways to help educators progress from understanding diversity to appreciating diversity through critical review of information regarding the diverse nature of students today. In Chapter 5, we discuss activities to engage educators moving from critical cultural awareness to transformative actions through dynamic culturally responsive interactions with students.

First, we revisit the concept of student diversity to establish the foundation for why it is so important for educators to move from understanding to appreciation. Then we offer different approaches and specific activities to enhance educators' knowledge, skills, and dispositions regarding student diversity.

From Understanding Diversity to Appreciating Diversity

In the Introduction of this book, we discussed the increasing diversity of students in P–12 settings, and highlighted the intricacy of diversity where multiple facets of diversity interact and overlap to form students' unique cultural identities, thus, impacting their multicultural development. Recognizing the complexity of this thing we call diversity, we view student diversity as the dynamic interconnectedness of visible, invisible, seen, unseen, recognized, and unrecognized individual and group identities that may lead to potential social marginalization and lack of equity in education. It is particularly important to note that while certain labels for diversity (such as race or English as a second language [ESL]) may be visible, seen, and recognized more easily by us as educators, other interconnected aspects of one's identity (such as socioeconomic status) also play an important role in our work with diverse student populations. We also acknowledge that when working with diverse students, educators must develop awareness, understanding, appreciation, and critical cultural awareness and then take transformative actions. The goal of the professional development that facilitates such cross-cultural interaction between educators and students, therefore, is to foster educators' ability to

- understand the varieties of diversity as well as strategies to enlarge their scope of knowledge;
- appreciate the sociocultural values associated with diversity;

- be critically aware and mindful in our cross-cultural interactions to monitor power relations; and
- imagine the alternatives to engage in transformative action for equity in education.

In this chapter, we focus our discussion on the first two goals, understanding and appreciating, before focusing in the next chapter on the latter two goals.

In most professional development sessions concentrating on diverse learners, educators have opportunities to enhance their knowledge of specific cultural groups. Taking various religious groups as an example, we know that religious membership identification is complex because there are many major and minor religious groups in the United States, and "Americans tend to identify not only with major groups" (Gollnick & Chinn, 2004, p. 224). With the growing religious pluralism and the impact of religion on people's values and beliefs, it is not only important for educators to understand and be knowledgeable about the general value system and traditions associated with each religious group but also be sensitive to the denominational differences within religious groups. Such knowledge would help educators determine what is appropriate and inappropriate language and behavior when interacting with students from various religious backgrounds. Of course, as we mentioned earlier in this book, it is impossible for us to provide any comprehensive description of all religious groups. Therefore, in professional development, it is more important that we equip educators with strategies to enhance their current knowledge through critical reflection as they encounter changing diversity among their students.

Besides building their knowledge about student diversity, educators also need to master perspective taking and be aware of the sociocultural values associated with diversity to develop an appreciation for diverse student backgrounds. Appreciation is different from understanding in that it involves dispositions and goes beyond knowledge. The word *appreciation* here carries two meanings: (1) affirmation with and empathy for the beliefs and values of diverse student populations and (2) individual self-evaluation about assumptions, biases, and stereotypes about diversity that lead to inequity in education. Through appreciation, educators can start to see that our knowledge *about* diversity is not neutral or matter-of-fact. Rather, it reflects the underlying assumptions and social oppression that need to be questioned or challenged. In the following section, we share some activities and resources for developing educators' knowledge and dispositions regarding student diversity.

ACTIVITY 4.1 DIVERSITY FACT SHEETS

Because of the complexity inherent in students' diverse backgrounds, educators need to know where and how to learn more about their students' cultural communities. As the name suggests, Diversity Fact Sheets display a collection of information about certain groups. The diversity groups can be defined by national origins, ethnicity, religion, special needs, and the like. Educators typically are asked to collect information from online sources to represent their growing understanding about a diversity group of their choice. Instead of trying to accumulate all the available information online, they are expected to review the available information, select what is relevant and applicable for teaching, represent the information in a concise format, and include classroom-teaching applications where applicable. With the improved accessibility of web-based technology, more and more information is updated and shared online, including information about diverse groups. Various organizations and associations have established websites to share their unique values, beliefs, and practices from different perspectives. However, it is important to remind educators at the outset to check and double-check the authenticity of the websites they explore and to gather information from multiple sources to triangulate what may be factual and what may be biased. The process of completing this activity helps educators not only identify online resources regarding diversity but also evaluate and examine their assumptions and potential biases.

When used in professional development with a group of educators, the group can determine what diversity groups they would like to learn more about based on their students' backgrounds or on areas of expertise they would like to develop. Then, specific diversity groups can be assigned to each educator, and the final fact sheets can be combined to create a portfolio for all educators to use. In addition to information sharing, after completing the fact sheets, it is important for educators to share their critical review of the online information so they could develop critical awareness of any potential biases and stereotypes of certain diversity groups.

Objectives

- To learn something about a student they do not know much about but whom they might have (or have had) in their classroom or school
- To critically evaluate and select information regarding diversity groups
- To share that information and their critical review with their peers

Instruction to Participants

Each participant will research at least one diversity group and develop a two-page fact sheet. These diversity groups may include various ethnicities, religions, exceptionalities, and so on. Participants will explore online resources and carefully evaluate and select relevant materials regarding the diversity group they have chosen. A fact sheet titled "What an Educator Should Know About _____" (e.g., Mexico, gifted students, or Seventh Day Adventists) will be developed for each research topic and will be shared. Use Resource 4.1 *Ideas for Factsheets: Collaboratively Generated by the Group With the Facilitator* on companion website for this book to help generate ideas about topics to select from.

Resource 4.2 *Sample Fact Sheets About Venezuela, Scientology, and GAD* is also located on companion website for this book to provide examples.

Suggestions/Background for Facilitation

When we do this fact sheet project with groups of 20 to 30 participants, all participants benefit because they end up with background information and useful tips and resources for 20 to 30 different ethnic groups, religions, and exceptionalities—and they also have the opportunity to practice their online research and computer skills. However, it is important to remind educators of the criteria to evaluate online resources (authority, objectivity, authenticity, reliability, timeliness, and relevance) and to be mindful of the language they choose to use when summarizing the information they gather.

Further, we usually ask participants to help brainstorm a list of ideas for what should be included in the fact sheets, as well as a list of possible diversity groups they might want to learn more about. Although we provide ideas for what should be included in Fact Sheets in Handout 4.1, this list should start with suggestions from educators and then be supplemented by the facilitator based on the ideas we provide.

Recommended Questions Following the Activity (I=Individual Reflection Questions, G=Group Discussion Questions)

- Why did you select the particular group to focus on for the fact sheet project? (I)
- How did you locate, evaluate, select, and summarize the information for the fact sheet project? (I & G)
- How did you resolve any conflicting information you found during your research? (I, G)
- What were your major findings? What surprised you? (I & G)
- How would you use the information on the fact sheet as an educator? (I & G)
- What have you learned from this process of developing the fact sheets as an educator? (I)

(Continued)

(Continued)

Debriefing Note

This activity provides educators not only with information regarding various diversity groups but, more important, with ways to gain background knowledge about a particular cultural group. Educators need such skills to continue learning about their students' diverse backgrounds because we will never have an exhaustive list of all the information we need to know about student diversity. In addition, the evaluation of the information we glean from online resources is critical. While gathering facts and information, as educators, we need to be mindful of any potential biases and stereotypes that might be associated with certain cultural groups, consciously aware of the range of diversity within every cultural group, and especially thoughtful about the language we use to describe group characteristics.

Time

- It takes 30 to 60 minutes for sharing and debriefing, but it requires extra time for participants to complete the fact sheets.

ACTIVITY 4.2 WEBSITE REVIEWS

Besides collecting information from multiple websites to enhance our understanding of a particular diversity group, educators can also conduct website reviews not only to gather information but also to evaluate the quality and usability of resources, services, and networks available on the websites. Educators with both the knowledge of available online resources and services for diverse groups and the understanding of how to evaluate and appreciate such resources are going to serve as better advocates for diverse student groups.

With the increasing use of technology in our daily lives, more and more people use websites to disseminate information, provide support services, and generate networks online. Educators can benefit from the content on these websites and also have the opportunity to become more connected with different communities online. Colorín Colorado (www.colorincolorado.org/), for example, is a bilingual website that offers support, resources, and information for educators, librarians, and families in both Spanish and English. The reading tips, activities, and free downloadable materials are great resources for students to engage in family literacy activities. Webcasts, videos, and podcasts are also provided on specific topics related to ESL teaching and learning. Educators can also sign up for free e-newsletters and share questions and suggestions through the website.

Even though there are many great websites available, the quality and usability of the sites vary significantly. Besides identifying useful aspects of the websites, as we have mentioned before, it is very important for educators to better understand how to evaluate the quality and usability of online information and become more informed and savvy users of the Internet. Practicing skills for evaluating websites will also facilitate those educators who might have or will develop classroom websites to extend their connections with students and families.

Objectives

- To synthesize information and resources available through online resources
- To identify ways to use online resources, information, and services to better understand students' backgrounds and meet their needs
- To critically evaluate the quality and use of various websites and become more informed users

Instruction to Participants

Form groups of three or four. Review the criteria for evaluating websites, and identify the criteria your group wants to use. Each member of the group selects one website from Resource 4.3 *Website List of Resources for Fact Sheets,* located on the companion website for this book, or identifies another website he or she would like to explore.

Synthesize the information and evaluate the quality and use of the website using Resource 4.4 *Format for Website Review Handout,* also found on the companion website for this book. Discuss with your group members and be prepared to share your thoughts with the whole group.

Suggestions/Background for Facilitation

You may choose to establish criteria for the website review activity as a whole group using the resources provided in the Online Extension section at the end of this chapter. Allow participants to use Resource 4.3 as a starting point and search for websites that they are interested in. Update the list with good websites participants find. To keep updated on websites regarding cultural diversity, you may want to join online listservs or associations such as the Multimedia Educational Resource for Learning and Online Teaching (MERLOT) at www.merlot.org, which offers peer reviews of many different kinds of websites and learning objects.

Recommended Questions Following the Activity (I=Individual Reflection Questions, G=Group Discussion Questions)

- Which aspects of the websites do you find most valuable as an educator? (I)
- How would the information we/you learned from the websites facilitate our/your teaching and learning in diverse settings? (I, G)

(Continued)

(Continued)

- What assumptions and values are associated with the different cultural groups based on your review? What information might be misleading? (I, G)
- How could we best use web resources in our teaching and learning about diversity? What are some cautions we need to take when we do that? (I, G)

Debriefing Note

Web resources are valuable in developing our understanding of different cultural groups. However, we need to be mindful in our use of such information. Depending on the sources and purposes of the websites, different assumptions, values, biases, and sometimes stereotypes may be presented. As educators, we not only need to know how to use such resources but also we need to be thoughtful in introducing web resources to our students in P–12.

Time

- It takes 60 to 90 minutes for reviewing and debriefing.

ACTIVITY 4.3 INTERACTIVE SURVEY

If diversity fact sheets and website reviews are activities for educators to get to know more about diversity groups, then interactive surveys are good ways to learn about individual students with whom we work. Many survey tools are available for educators to use in identifying students' multiple intelligences, learning styles, and motivational factors. The results of these surveys allow educators to identify learner preferences, and this information can be helpful when educators design class activities and assessments. Further, for older students, completing these kinds of survey instruments helps them develop metacognitive awareness of their preferences in learning and become more intentional in developing habits to maximize their efficiency in learning.

It is worth noting that student survey measures have also been developed based on positive psychology theories. Taking a strength-based perspective, these instruments emphasize the identification of the assets and strengths that students bring to the classroom. Instead of focusing on the gaps that need to be filled or the problems that need to be solved, the strength-based perspective allows educators to focus on students' potential. For students coming from diverse cultural and linguistic backgrounds, this is especially important for several reasons. First, because various cultural values and beliefs diverse students have might differ from traditional mainstream expectations at the school, some of their strengths and assets may not be recognized. For example, students from many Asian countries may value harmony rather than individual opinion in group discussions. Without recognizing such value systems, students' classroom behavior may easily be interpreted as being passive in group work or as a lack of English language proficiency. Second, many students from culturally and linguistically diverse backgrounds would benefit from having enhanced self-efficacy for learning. The identification of their unique strengths and assets would help the students evaluate themselves from a different perspective and learn to leverage their strengths in learning. Finally, the use of strength-based instruments would also help educators reconsider the kinds of activities and assignments needed to build on students' background and their strengths.

Although survey results may provide us with information about our students, we also need to be aware that students' learning styles, attitudes, motivations, even their strengths will change over time. It would be ideal if educators could develop an ongoing system for getting to know their students, rather than simply relying on one or two instruments or activities at the beginning of the semester. Portfolio assessment is a good example of such an ongoing assessment system. LinguaFolio (www.ncssfl.org/links/index.php?linguafolio), for example, is a student portfolio assessment system focusing on students' language background. It typically includes three components: (1) passport, where formal assessments of student language proficiency and students' self-assessment are included; (2) biography, where information regarding students' language background, language learning experiences, and cross-cultural activities are documented; and (3) dossier, where samples of students' work over time are archived. This type of assessment system makes students' transition from one teacher to another, or one school to another, much easier. It also empowers the students as they are put in charge of selecting and documenting their progress in learning.

In Resource 4.5 *Resources for Survey Instruments*, located in companion website for this book, sample survey instruments measuring multiple intelligences, learning styles, motivation, self-efficacy, strengths, and assets are provided. However, it is important to note that the use of these survey instruments may require school, district, and parent approval. Educators need to be mindful in selecting the appropriate measure that is not only informative but also beneficial for students and families involved. With the use of any survey instrument, we always need to consider its reliability, validity, and cultural sensitivity. No matter how widely used some of these instruments are, it is always a good idea for educators to carefully examine the survey items before using the instruments with their students. This activity, therefore, is designed for educators to try and to evaluate some of the survey instruments they may consider using with their students. Through this activity, educators may also develop insights regarding potential cultural bias in assessments.

(Continued)

(Continued)

Objectives

- To learn how to use survey instruments to get to know students better
- To interpret survey data to modify instruction that better meet students' needs
- To evaluate survey items to identify potential cultural biases

Recommended Use

Also, some of the surveys in Resource 4.5 can be used as a tool for facilitators to better know what participants in their professional development sessions bring to the discussion. Once participants have completed the surveys and discussed their uses, they can be encouraged to consider applying them with the students they work with as well. It is important to remind educators obtaining appropriate approval before adopting any survey instruments for use with students.

Instruction to Participants

Select one of the survey instruments from Resource 4.5 that participants may not be familiar with. Have participants complete the survey during the session or as homework. Pair participants and ask them to review each other's survey results. Have participants answer questions listed on Resource 4.6 *Instructions for Interpreting Survey Results*, also located on the companion website for this book, as they review the survey results. Share the responses with a partner or in a small group.

Recommended Questions Following the Activity (I=Individual Reflection Questions, G=Group Discussion Questions)

- How do you like the instrument you completed? Does it reflect your background or what you thought you knew about yourself? (I)
- How did you interpret the survey results? Were your interpretations validated? (I)
- How would you use this instrument with your students? Are there any items you would like to change or modify? Why? (I & G)

Debriefing Note

You may also decide to modify the survey instruments to better reflect the focus of the course or professional development. Participants could also be encouraged to share some survey instruments they have found or questions they typically ask their students to better get to know them. However, the process of evaluating and interpreting the instrument is critical in this activity. It is important to discuss ways to search for patterns based on survey responses and how these responses could further guide instructional decision making. The possibility of using survey instruments as formative assessment tools should also be discussed. Discussion of assessment validity and reliability may emerge as a key point through this activity. Educators should be encouraged to evaluate the cultural sensitivity of survey items.

Time

- This activity takes 30 to 45 minutes.

ACTIVITY 4.4 DESCRIPTION, INTERPRETATION, AND EVALUATION

As we start to get to know our students through direct interactions (through conducting an interactive survey, for example), we need to be very conscientious of our assumptions and potential biases as we interpret and evaluate such interactions. Our dialogue with students is a constructive process where we start to form or build a student profile in our mind, oftentimes in a subconscious manner. Through this process, it is inevitable that we add our beliefs and prior experiences to fill in the blanks to make our picture of students more complete and meaningful for us. Because of the interpretive nature of such profile building, we may misinterpret or misevaluate our students because our understanding is often limited by our scope of knowledge and prior experiences.

This is especially true when we may not be fully aware of the cultural or linguistic backgrounds of the students we are working with. For example, the following is how a teacher recalls her impression of a student in her class:

He is an introvert and quiet child. He does not talk much in class. When we are doing fun activities in class, he seldom laughs with the other kids. I am a little worried about his ability to socialize with other children. In our art class, he does not participate in any drawing activity. I think he understands the instruction, but he just refuses to draw. I am a little frustrated with him, and I am not sure how to make him understand that he needs to show respect to teachers in all his classes.

Although this teacher's account appears to be observational, further analysis indicates that not all the information presented here is descriptive and that some of it is the writer's interpretation or evaluation. To demonstrate how to do a careful analysis of our observations, we use solid underline to indicate description; the dashed underline represents teacher interpretation; and the wave underline indicates the teacher's evaluation. The teacher observes, "He does not talk much in class," "he seldom laughs with the other kids," and "he does not participate in any drawing activity." She interprets the observed behaviors as the student being "introverted and quiet" and "refuses to draw." Based on the interpretation, the teacher was very

(Continued)

(Continued)

concerned about his social skills and lack of respect. These are definitely logical inter-pretations, and the teacher's concerns may be legitimate. However, if we stop here without consciously distinguishing between description, interpretation, and evalua-tion in our account, or if we do not further explore possible alternative interpretations, this type of account might prevent us from seeing perspectives other than ours. This can mislead us to draw biased conclusions regarding the student's behavior.

In this particular case, the teacher questioned her initial interpretation and evaluation and talked with the student and others who have worked with the student to learn more about his prior learning experiences and cultural back-ground. As a result, she was able to reach alternative interpretations based on the observation that the student did not think it was appropriate to laugh in class because of his prior school expectations, and he did not feel comfortable drawing for the teacher because he felt that he lacked the skills to do a good job at it. This alternative interpretation allowed the teacher to keep an open mind when observ-ing and interacting further with the student in class to monitor his development and transition into the U.S. school system.

This example illustrates the importance of educators having the skills to reflect on and distinguish among description, interpretation, and evaluation during their interactions with students. The following activity, which we adapted from Lustig and Koester (2003), is one way we have used to purposefully guide educators to be more reflective during both observations and interactions and to develop skills in seeking alternative interpretations and evaluations in their work with diverse students.

Objectives

- To distinguish between description, interpretation, and evaluation
- To seek alternative interpretations based on our observations and interac-tions with students

Recommended Use

If participants are not familiar with the distinction between description, inter-pretation, and evaluation, this activity is best done in a face-to-face setting with a group discussion, perhaps using a video or a similar written scenario. Then, participants can be encouraged to apply the process to their daily interactions and observations of students. Follow-up sharing could be conducted either face-to-face or through online discussions.

Instruction to Participants

Ask participants to think about a student they worked with in the last week, and write a brief paragraph about the student. Tell participants to save that paragraph for later use in the session. Next, the facilitator shares an ambiguous object or picture with participants (for example, a picture of a student falling asleep during class) and asks the participants to, "Tell me something about this picture." Allow participants one to two minutes to think about it and then share their thoughts. The facilitator records participants' responses and purposefully separates description, interpretation, and evaluation statements into three different columns on the board without labeling them.

The facilitator then asks participants what they see in common among the statements that were recorded within the same column, and guides participants to distinguish between description, interpretation, and evaluation. It might also help to add sentence starters to clarify. For example, the facilitator might use these labels: description (I see/observe), interpretation (I think/believe), and evaluation (I feel) to make it very clear how important it is to discuss how we might reach different interpretations and evaluations.

Ask participants to review the paragraph they wrote at the beginning of the session and distinguish between description, interpretation, and evaluation. Pair participants so they can facilitate each other in reaching alternative interpretations and evaluations.

Suggestions/Background for Facilitation

In this activity, some participants may feel judged because their initial interpretation or evaluation of the student may not be "right." It is important for the facilitator to emphasize that the point of the process is not to judge whether we come up with the right or wrong interpretation. Instead, we are trying to learn how we can keep an open mind so we are not easily trapped into one way of thinking and not be able to see from alternative perspectives. To mitigate concerns about being judged, facilitators may want to share their account of a student and model self-analysis to demonstrate the self-reflection process and make participants more comfortable in engaging in the activity. As an alternative, facilitators can offer their personal experiences for participants to practice analyzing description, interpretation, and evaluation rather than having participants using their accounts.

Recommended Questions Following the Activity (I=Individual Reflection Questions, G=Group Discussion Questions)

- What is the most challenging part in this exercise? (I, G)
- How do you reach alternative interpretations? (I)
- How could we apply this process in our daily interactions with students? (G)

Time

- This activity takes 30 to 45 minutes.

SUMMARY OF KEY POINTS

In this chapter, we focused on ideas and activities to engage educators in the development of their understanding and appreciation of the diversity of our P–12 students to assist in their development of critical cultural awareness and competence in meeting the needs of diverse learners.

- We defined the complex nature of cultural identity as the dynamic interconnectedness of various individual and group identities that may lead to potential social marginalization and inequitable education.
- We distinguished between educators' understanding and appreciation of student diversity because we believe that effective professional development needs to engage educators in activities that move them beyond just knowledge regarding various diversity groups. Educators need to be able to develop affirmation with and empathy for diversity and to critically evaluate the sociocultural values, assumptions, and biases associated with the information shared about diversity. Four specific activities are shared:
  - Activity 4.1 Diversity Fact Sheets
  - Activity 4.2 Website Reviews
  - Activity 4.3 Interactive Survey
  - Activity 4.4 Description, Interpretation, and Evaluation

REFLECTION AND EXTENSION

- Reflect on the activities and assignments you have done in the past. What are some ideas you have to engage educators in developing their understanding of student diversity?
- How would you modify these activities and assignments to move educators from understanding to appreciation of diversity?
- If you were to compose a metaphor about student diversity, what would it be?

ONLINE EXTENSIONS

If educators need additional support in using the Internet for research and for creating high-quality fact sheets and conducting website

reviews, some of the many places they can go to learn about how to
evaluate the accuracy of online information include the following:

- *Five Criteria for Evaluating Websites* from Cornell University at
  www.library.cornell.edu/olinuris/ref/research/webcrit
  .html
- The *Evaluating Internet Resources* page from Teacher Tap-
  Professional Development Resources for Educators and Librarians
  at http://eduscapes.com/tap/topic32.htm
- Links to criteria that assist educators and students to critically
  evaluate online resources from Kathy Schrock's Guide for
  Educators at http://school.discoveryeducation.com/schrock
  guide/eval.html

Both the fact sheets and the website reviews can easily be used as
part of the requirements for online professional development sessions
and readily shared with the entire online community. Fact sheets can be
posted as PDFs that educators can download and print to share further.
Participants could contribute their website reviews to a wiki page
designed with a particular focus related to the content of the professional development session (for example, assessment accommodations
for diverse learners, vocabulary strategies for English Learners [ELs],
or culturally responsive teaching practices). Schools that have or want
to develop resource web pages for teachers, parents, and students
could also use this activity to involve educators in providing ongoing
input to update information regarding online resources.

FOCUS FOR PROFESSIONAL LEARNING COMMUNITIES (PLCs)

Enhancing educators' knowledge of the diverse student groups they
work with could be an identified focus for various PLCs. Through collaboration, educators could not only share resources and knowledge
but also develop critical thinking in using resources. When using the
fact sheet or website review activities, we would recommend that educators start with brainstorming questions and/or concerns they might
have regarding particular cultural groups based on the profile of the
students they are interacting with. Then, they could assign tasks to
complete components of the fact sheet or website review in pairs or
individually and bring the results back to share with the PLCs. During
their sharing, the discussion questions could be used to reflect critically on the quality and the use of identified resources, as well as on

the range of diversity within the topics they researched. The tips for instruction aspects of the fact sheets will be especially valuable if members of the PLC all agree to try some of them.

For the interactive surveys and the description, interpretation, evaluation activities, we would encourage educators to complete the activities during PLC discussions, reflect on how they could use what they learned in their interactions with the students, and then actually apply it in their teaching contexts. Reflections on their experiences of applying the survey or the description, interpretation, and evaluation process can then be shared at the follow-up PLC sessions.

5

From Critical Awareness to Transformative Action

How Do We Prepare Educators to Become Cultural Brokers for Student Success?

Introduction

Students, especially those with different linguistic and cultural backgrounds, are always learning to negotiate between their personal identity, family culture, and the culture of their classrooms and schools. In this learning process, educators usually play dual roles. As professionals facilitating the reinforcement of school policies and regulations, as well as classroom rules and expectations, educators are integral members of the school culture. Educators in most schools have shared understandings and perceptions that guide common classroom routines and practices at those schools. However, educators who work with students from diverse cultural backgrounds also need to be able to play the role of *cultural brokers*, serving as the bridge or link between different cultural groups and as an advocate for individuals or groups (Jezewski & Sotnik, 2001). Educators' cultural brokering not only occurs between individual students and the school, but among various student cultural groups within the class as well. Although understanding and appreciating student diversity is important for educators to successfully serve as cultural brokers, it is not enough. Educators also need to become critically aware and mindful in monitoring their interactions with students, as well as the interactions among students. Further, educators who are critically culturally competent need to take a step further to challenge the status quo and be willing to imagine alternatives to enhance equity in education.

In this chapter, we focus our discussion on critical cultural awareness and transformative actions for educators to serve as cultural brokers for their students. Activities and strategies for moving us beyond an understanding and appreciation of diversity are provided.

From Critical Awareness to Transformative Action

As more and more educators enter teaching from various cultural backgrounds and with different cross-cultural experiences, they acknowledge the importance of valuing and integrating students' diverse cultural backgrounds in daily instruction. However, proper disposition is just the first step to successful cross-cultural interactions with students and families. Educators also need to develop skills to monitor their critical cultural awareness that leads to transformative actions in teaching.

Given the current curriculum, standards, and school learning environment, there are a number of areas educators need to be working on to better promote equity in education and provide opportunities for students to cherish, develop, and leverage their cultural assets for both academic and cultural identity development (Gay, 2010; Ladson-Billings, 2001). A vital component of educators' critical cultural competence lies in their abilities to act as agents of change (Villegas & Lucas, 2002). Instead of being content with using good teaching strategies, educators with critical cultural competence question how they can become better cultural brokers in and beyond the classrooms. In addition to their individual development of cultural awareness, they are concerned about the cultural sensitivity of peers, parents, and students they work with. They are committed to and engaged in ongoing curriculum and school reforms that transform the way we build home–school connections, view student achievement and learning, and measure student success in school settings.

In their efforts to challenge the status quo and become more critically culturally competent by leading the change in their interactions with curriculum, students, and parents, inevitably, educators will face barriers and obstacles. To sustain their transformative actions as change agents, educators need to develop not only a sense of agency (Fairbanks et al., 2010) and agency thinking, but "pathways thinking" as well (Snyder, 1995, p. 355). Discussing the process that leads to future development and change, Snyder (1995) defined one's hope as "the process of thinking about one's goals, along with the motivation to move toward those goals (agency), and the ways to achieve those goals (pathways)" (p. 355). For educators who are committed to promoting equity in education, they not only need to be motivated for doing so, but more important, they need to learn ways to seek alternative strategies and to develop resilience throughout the process.

Toward these ends, we provide professional development activities and projects that engage educators in the development of both agency and pathways thinking in real-world, cross-cultural interactions as "much of what teachers need to learn must be learned in and from practice rather than preparing for practice" (Zeichner, 2010, p. 91).

Cross-Cultural Competence and Critical Self-Reflection

Both educators' experiences with cross-cultural interactions and their ongoing reflections are inseparable components in their critical cultural competence development. In the three activities described in this chapter, we not only provide guidelines for educators to engage in the projects but also specify the accompanying reflective activities. Sample reflections from educators who have completed these projects are also shared.

ACTIVITY 5.1 ACTIVE LISTENING

Direct interaction with students is one of the most critical ways for educators to build relationships with their students. Although, as educators, we have the opportunity to listen to students every day, we do not necessarily use these opportunities to interact with our students and learn about and from them. Developing and using active listening skills allows educators to be more purposeful and mindful in their interactions with students, and it enhances the effectiveness of our daily communications. The purposes of active listening are to focus listeners' attention

(Continued)

(Continued)

on the speakers' message and to develop a clear mutual understanding of shared information or concerns. This is especially important in our work with culturally and linguistically diverse students. Coming from different cultural and linguistic backgrounds than their students, teachers and administrators need to monitor the verbal and nonverbal cues that may carry specific meanings in different cultures. For example, some students may avoid making direct eye contact with the teacher in an effort to show respect. Also, we need to be aware of the potential assumptions and biases we may carry as we interpret students' verbal or nonverbal behaviors. To empower students to develop skills in cross-cultural communication, educators also need to be explicit in modeling and teaching active listening strategies in their classrooms and schools.

Active listening involves specific skills that allow us to attend to the speaker and suspend our frame of references and assumptions. Focusing on culturally appropriate interpersonal communication skills, Ivey and Ivey (2007), for example, detailed attending behavior and basic listening strategies. According to Ivey and Ivey, attending behavior includes proper visual/eye contact, vocal qualities, verbal tracking, and body language (3Vs + B). Our cultural backgrounds impact how we choose to keep or break eye contact in conversation, use body language to facilitate conversation or convey subtle messages, and display and react to certain accents, pitches, and volume in conversations. We also develop patterns in selecting certain messages to pay attention to (i.e., selective attention) and ignore others. Being mindful of our attending behavior patterns and keen on observing our students would help us become more effective in demonstrating attending behavior in cross-cultural communications. In addition to attending behavior, listening skills involve ways of questioning, observing, paraphrasing, and reflecting on feelings (Ivey & Ivey, 2007). Although these may be perceived as trivial aspects in communications, they are critical skills that enhance the quality of cross-cultural interactions.

Objectives

- To practice active listening skills
- To monitor our verbal and nonverbal behavior patterns in cross-cultural communication
- To become more sensitive and skillful in using attending behaviors and active listening strategies

Instruction to Participants

Before the activity, think about a student, a teacher, an administrator, or a parent you really enjoyed talking with. List as many attributes as you can think of that make your conversations smooth for you. (Facilitators may want to share their personal examples first to model and lead the discussion.) Summarizing participants' experiences after their sharing, the facilitator will introduce Ivey and Ivey's (2007) 3Vs + B model and discuss potential cultural differences using Resource 5.1 *Attending Behavior and Active Listening* (Ivey & Ivey, 2007), located on the companion website for this book.

Grouping

Assign participants into groups of three. Each group needs to have a speaker, a listener, and an observer. You can have more listeners or observers in each group if needed.

Activity Tasks in Groups

- Speakers will have three minutes to share a communication experience where misunderstandings were involved.
- Listeners will use active listening strategies including both verbal and nonverbal behaviors to clarify, encourage, paraphrase, and summarize the conversation.
- Observers will use Resource 5.2: *Feedback Form for Attending Behavior (adapted from Ivey & Ivey, 2007)*, also located on the companion website for this book, to record the observation.

Recommended Questions Following the Activity (I=Individual Reflection Questions, G=Group Discussion Questions)

After the activity, regroup participants into three groups so all speakers, listeners, and observers are together. Have each group discuss the first two questions and then reflect individually in writing about the last two questions:

- What are some nonverbal and verbal behaviors that facilitated the conversation? (G)
- What areas of diversity in communication patterns have you noticed through this activity? (G)
- What did you learn about communication from the 3Vs + B exercise? (I)
- What did you learn about yourself based on this exercise? (I)

Time

- This activity and discussion takes 30 to 45 minutes.

Another framework that facilitators may consider using is the LAFF Don't CRY strategy (McNaughton & Vostal, 2010). In their article describing the way in which active listening strategies were used to improve teacher collaboration with parents,

(Continued)

(Continued)

McNaughton and Vostal (2010) described this strategy and provided examples of how educators could use it:

Listen, empathize, and communicate respect
Ask questions and ask permission to take notes
Focus on the issues
Find a first step

Don't

Criticize
React hastily and promise something you cannot deliver
Yakety-yak-yak

Facilitators could introduce this framework and use the example in the article to have participants label the strategies used. Participants could then be asked to reflect on potential cultural differences and practice using the strategies in real conversations.

Potential Challenges

One of the major challenges for successful delivery of this activity is facilitator's scaffolding of the discussion on various cultural patterns that impact verbal and nonverbal behaviors. It is important that the facilitator be able to build on what participants bring from their unique cultural backgrounds, as well as bring any subconscious behaviors a conscious level for additional debriefing. Depending on participants' knowledge of cultural and communication patterns, in addition to the Ivey and Ivey (2007) book and McNaughton and Vostal (2010) article, the facilitator may choose to use materials from other online resources listed in Online Extensions at the end of the chapter. During the discussion, it is also important for the facilitator to note any potential stereotypical assumptions participants may hold. A discussion of individual differences in verbal and nonverbal expressions within certain cultural groups might be also necessary.

ACTIVITY 5.2 CLASSROOM OBSERVATION ANALYSIS

Classroom observation analysis is another way for educators to monitor their interaction with students and examine potential cultural biases or behavioral patterns that may prohibit students from full participation in class discussions and learning. Different from traditional observation of other teachers' classrooms, the purpose of the observation analysis is not necessarily learning new teaching strategies or ways to manage the classroom. Rather, it provides educators with an opportunity to observe students' behaviors in their classroom or school learning environment and to learn about their various reactions and interaction patterns.

The observation can be done in other teachers' classrooms, through watching a video demonstration lesson, or by watching a recorded lesson of one's instruction of or interactions with students in various contexts. The focus of the observation needs to be identified, especially with real-time observations because it is impossible for us to observe and note everything that is going on in our classrooms and schools. For example, some educators may be curious about how boys and girls participate in math instruction differently. In their observation, they may decide to focus on the frequency in which boys and girls participate in class discussions, the types of questions they choose to respond to, different ways they use manipulatives to solve problems, and the like. During the observation, they take detailed notes and record any comments or questions they may have. When discussing or writing about their observations, they are cautioned to try to separate their description (what was observed), interpretation (what they think happened), and evaluation (what they think are positive and/or negative aspects of the observation), as was discussed previously in Chapter 4.

Engaging in such analysis allows educators to have an opportunity to learn from students' authentic interactions to guide and enhance the quality of their education in the future. In addition, being an observer in the classroom, rather than the teacher, offers a unique perspective for educators to question some hidden assumptions and learn to become more sensitive to the needs of diverse student populations. Finally, the observation analysis project could also be adapted and used for mentoring, peer coaching, or as part of a project to engage educators in action research projects. As one experienced teacher commented after completing the project, "I personally feel that I got a lot out of the experience of completing the observation analysis paper because it gave me a direction to focus on within my own classroom and school."

Objectives

- To focus on student interactions in classroom observation
- To reflect on our assumptions and potential cultural conflicts for students coming from diverse cultural backgrounds;
- To engage in mentoring, peer coaching, or action research projects based on observation and analysis

Instruction to Participants

For this classroom observation analysis, you will do the following:

- Identify a focus for observation
  - What would you like to learn about student interactions in the classroom? Why?
  - Why do you want to observe in this particular classroom setting?
  - What do you expect to learn from the observation?

(Continued)

(Continued)

- Provide a description of the observation
  - ○ What does the setting look like?
  - ○ Who are the people (teachers, administrators, staff, students) involved? How many of them? How are they seated?
  - ○ Provide detailed notes of interactions between teacher and students, teachers and their assistants or other teachers, administrator and students, students and students, and so on. You can also focus your observation on one particular student or one particular instructional activity (teacher feedback, for example).
- Share your interpretation of the observation
  - ○ What do you think happened based on your observation?
- Share your evaluation of the observation
  - ○ Based on your knowledge, what are some positive aspects of the classroom interactions observed?
  - ○ Are there any aspects that need improvement or things you may have questions about?
- Reflect on your teaching
  - ○ What have you learned from this observation?
  - ○ What are some assumptions we may need to be mindful of when working with students who have diverse backgrounds?

Recommended Questions Following the Activity (I=Individual Reflection Questions, G=Group Discussion Questions)

Participants may choose to work on the observation project individually or in small groups, and they can then share their reflections as a large group. If participants are using this activity as part of the mentoring program, where the mentor and mentee have ongoing observations of each other's classrooms and follow-up discussions, they may also want to discuss various instructional approaches they may use to better address the needs of all students and identify the focus of the next observation based on the discussion.

Time

- Depending on the time spent on observation and whether the analyses are shared in an oral or a written format, this activity may take three hours to more than one day to complete.

Resource 5.3 *Sample Observation Form*, located on the companion website for this book, offers a useful format for completing this classroom-observation analysis project. In addition to the narrative observation notes, some educators may also want to tally the frequency of specific interactions observed. One teacher who was interested in exploring the patterns of teacher questioning and feedback to

boys versus girls in class, for example, categorized the observed interactions and recorded the frequency using this format.

	Boys	Girls
Number of questions asked	9	7
Number of feedback provided	9	5
Questions—lower level (clarification, asking for para-phrase, repetition, etc.)	7	7
Questions—higher level	2	0
Feedback—no scaffolding (e.g., saying "good")	7	5
Feedback—with scaffolding (e.g., providing further assistance to achieve success in the question)	4	1

A simple frequency count allowed this teacher candidate to discover that "more difficult questions were asked to the males and more praise was given to them than to the females" during math instruction. Analyzing the potential assumptions the math teacher may hold, this teacher reflected that "if the teacher has a bias that boys are naturally better at mathematics, provides them with more scaffolding, and gives them more of a chance to succeed, then this will have negative ramifications for the girls in the class." As a follow-up to the observation analysis, this teacher shared his observation with other faculty at the school and planned on engaging faculty in discussions regarding enhancing teachers' awareness of such potential assumptions and biases.

Potential Challenges

For this activity, it is especially important that participants clearly identify the focus of their observations so they can use the observation data to answer questions they may have regarding the classroom interactions of students from culturally and linguistically diverse backgrounds. The facilitator may want to refer to the action research discussion in Chapter 3 for more ideas for guiding educators in focusing their observation, collection, and analysis of the observation data.

ACTIVITY 5.3 ABCs PROJECT

Bringing together ways to explore who we are as educators as well as ways to learn about and from our students, the ABCs Project involves educators' use of all these skills to enhance their self-knowledge and critical cultural competence from learning about self, learning about their students, and, most important, the comparison and combination of the two.

(Continued)

(Continued)

Schmidt (1999) developed the ABCs model to better prepare educators for bilingual and bicultural students. The model depicts a five-step process (Schmidt, 1999; 2001; Schmidt & Finkbeiner, 2006):

1. Autobiography, where educators write about their life stories
2. Biography, where educators conduct interviews, home visits, and observations to compose a biography of a student whose linguistic or cultural backgrounds are different
3. Cross-cultural analysis, through which educators examine the autobiography and biography and identify the similarities and differences
4. Appreciation of differences, which involves educators critical self-analysis of the cultural differences; and
5. Home/school/community connections for literacy development, where educators develop a plan to connect home, school, and community based on their ABCs study.

This model has been adapted for preservice teacher education programs (e.g., He & Cooper, 2009) and for inservice teachers' professional development as they modify content-area instruction for students with diverse backgrounds (Schmidt & Finkbeiner, 2006). Finkbeiner and Koplin (2002) also adapted the model for the European teaching context and applied it to teacher intercultural communication competence development internationally.

In our work with educators using the ABCs model, we noted their development in cultural competence as measured by the Cultural Diversity Attitude Inventory (He & Cooper, 2009). We observed that educators tended to feel "tentative toward the project" before starting, but after completing the project, many commented how they were "surprised at how much more comfortable they have become in cross-cultural communication in such a short amount of time." Those who perceived the project as easy, "as long as you speak the same language" as the students and their parents, also discovered that "even if we spoke the same language, cultural differences still existed." Further, educators coming from diverse cultural and linguistic backgrounds, themselves, were able to add much more to their autobiography at the end of the project and reflected more in-depth about their identity development process and ways they could empower their students and the families based on their personal experiences. After working with adult English Learners (ELs) who were young mothers for the ABCs Project, for example, one beginning educator designed "a model of teaching young moms about the practices and expectations of the public schools, including the pressures their children face to adopt the culture of their peers." She learned that

The parents are often at a loss when it comes to understanding the slang their kids pick up and the clothing they want to wear. As parents, they seem starved for a safe and understanding setting in which they can discuss such adjustment issues and receive feedback from teachers who understand their children's world as well as their own.

Objectives

- To explore and better understand our worldviews
- To learn from our students' cultures through interactions with students and families from diverse backgrounds
- To confront our biases as a means to better communicate and work with students and families

Instruction to Participants

We have used this adaptation of Schmidt's (1999) ABCs model with educators working with ELs. As a leader of professional development for a professional learning community (PLC) or a school, you may want to modify and adapt the specific questions that best match the local teaching contexts and your student population, which may or may not include ELs. For example, if the diversity in your school is mainly economic, you can adjust the questions accordingly.

Autobiography

As we start our work with our students, I think it will be very helpful to reflect on the experiences and beliefs that have shaped who we are as educators today. See the guiding questions the follow.

Thinking about your experience. Think about the cultural history of your family.

- Identify the people or experiences that you feel have shaped your cultural outlook.
- How are your values shaped? Which values do you wish to pass on to your children and your students? How?
- How do your school experience, the literature you read, and the media you are exposed to shape your cultural outlook?
- How has the culture in which you live changed?

Language and culture in your life. Think about your experiences communicating with people who are not native speakers of English and your foreign language learning experiences.

- What do you do when you do not understand people who speak a different language?
- Have you had misunderstandings in your communication (such as food, gestures, idioms, ritual and courtesy, touch and personal space)?

(Continued)

(Continued)

- Have you ever tried to learn a foreign language? When did you feel successful? What were the struggles you faced?
- What feelings/emotions do you associate with foreign language learning?

Who are you as an educator? Think about your experience as an educator interacting with ELs.

- How are ELs different from other students? What do you think educators need to do to best facilitate ELs' learning?
- What do you want to accomplish as an educator? Who do you want to see your ELs become?

Biography

To compose the biography of the student, you will need to

- identify a student whose cultural background is different from yours and who you have access to (you may need to ask for permission);
- get to know the student from both the school-based perspective and community-based perspective;
- collect information regarding students' cognitive and academic background, linguistic background, sociocultural background; and
- write a cohesive biography of the student.

Aspects you want to look into

	School Based	Community Based
Cognitive and academic background	• Prior schooling experiences • Academic proficiency (content-area assessment) • Learning styles • Learning strategies	• Academic access • Academic hope • Family literacy • Culturally relevant thinking and learning process
Linguistic background	• L1 proficiency • L2 proficiency • L2 learning experiences • Use of L2 in classroom settings	• L1 learning experiences • Use of L1 and L2 in social settings • L2 language attitude
Sociocultural background	• General family cultural background (parental education background, language experiences, etc.) • Content area interests	• Family values and cultural background • Community background and influence • Hopes and dreams

Sources for Information

- Parent interview
- Teacher interview
- Student interview
- Classroom observation
- Assignment analysis
- Home visits
- Community visits

Cross-Cultural Comparison

Comparing your experiences and what you know about the student you worked with, what are some similarities and differences in your family backgrounds, the communities in which you live, previous experiences, and academic learning experiences?

	Similarities	Differences
Cognitive and academic background		
Linguistic background		
Sociocultural background		

Cultural Differences Analysis

- Reflect on the biography and cross-cultural comparison
- Identify the possible cultural conflicts and/or differences between you and the student you worked with
- Explain any discomforts you or the student and his or her family may have experienced during the process
- Identify the impact of the project on both you and the student

Revised Autobiography

- Review your initial autobiography. What would you like to add or edit?
- What have you learned about yourself in terms of
  - o Your family background and cultural values
  - o Prior experiences and academic learning experiences
  - o Your role as an educator, especially in working with students from culturally and linguistically different backgrounds

(Continued)

(Continued)

Recommendations

- Provide recommendations and modifications for administrators and both regular classroom and specialist teachers at your school.
- Offer an action plan for successful communication among educators, students, and parents.

Recommended Questions Following the Activity (I=Individual Reflection Questions, G=Group Discussion Questions)

Because this individual project involves multiple steps, it is important for facilitators to engage participants in discussions to plan and reflect at each step. Resource 5.4 *Planning for the ABCs Project*, located on the companion website for this book, provides an example of potential questions facilitators could use to guide discussions of the project throughout the process. We have done this both through individual conferences and as group discussions held periodically throughout the time given to complete the ABCs Project.

Time

- This activity could be used as a project for a semester-long professional development series or undertaken by members of a PLC over the course of a few months.

Variations on the ABCs Project

In addition to the ABCs model described previously, many other researchers and educators also used narrative-based approaches for learning about the self and our students. Depending on the specific school contexts you are working in, the ABCs Project can be modified to maximize the learning of educators by completing different versions of this project. Three examples of how the ABCs Project could be modified and used in professional development are offered next. The instructions for participants are slightly different for each modification, but the objectives and recommended discussion questions remain the same.

Biography Cards Comparison (adapted from Herrera, 2010).

Herrera (2010) described ways to connect student biography and content area instruction in her recent book *Biography-Driven Culturally Responsive Teaching*. In her book, Herrera not only discussed the theoretical framework used for narrative inquiry to learn about students' background but also provided practical handouts educators could use in their interactions with students and during professional development, including the student biography card template, which we have used successfully. Using the student biography card and conducting biography comparisons could be an alternative to the ABCs Project, when there is not adequate time to the complete ABCs Project. Several additional templates and professional development handouts from Herrera's book can be found at www.tcpress .com/pdfs/0807750867.pdf.

Instruction for Participants

For this project, you will complete the following:

- Fill out the biography card (www.tcpress.com/pdfs/0807750867.pdf) based on your personal learning experiences.
- Identify a student you would like to learn more about and whose cultural background is likely to be different from yours.
- Fill out the biography card for the student through discussion with other teachers or staff working with the student, and search online for information relevant to the student's background.
- Add information to the biography card based on your observation of the student (in class, on the playground, or in other settings beyond classrooms) and/or direct interactions with the student (tutoring, reading together, talking during lunch or recess, etc.).
- Try to talk with family members of the student and add more information to the biography card. Ideally, it would be best to have a face-to-face conversation, but a telephone call would be fine.
- Compare your biography card with the student's, and compare information you obtained from different sources. What are similarities and differences?
- Write a reflection to summarize the similarities and differences you noted and what you learned in ways to get to know your particular student and other students as well.

ABC Group Project

This is another variation of the ABCs Project where pairs or groups of educators work together to learn more about one student and then compare their biographies with those of the student. This might be an ideal variation of the ABCs Project for a PLC to undertake with some of the students they are working hard to help.

Instruction for Participants

For this project, you will complete the following:

- Work together in groups of two to three people.
- Write your individual autobiography reflecting on your family background, learning experiences, and experiences interacting with people from other cultures.

(Continued)

(Continued)

- Identify a student you would like to learn more about and whose cultural background is likely to be different from yours.
- As a group, reflect on your autobiography and specify three to five questions you have about the student's family background and learning experiences (e.g., What is the language/dialect the student uses at home, with his or her siblings, or in classrooms? How is it similar to or different from what is used at school with the teacher?).
- As a group, discuss where you might obtain information about the student to answer those questions, and then proceed to learn about the student and his or her family and cultural background.
- Compose a biography about the student you work with as a group to focus on the questions you have; for those questions you could not answer, specify why you think they are hard to address. Keep in mind the differences among describing, interpreting, and evaluating information about students addressed in Chapter 4.
- Individually, write a reflection to summarize your contribution to the group project and reflect on how you could use what you learned through this project as an educator.

ABCs Project With Other Educators

In schools where there are educators from various cultural backgrounds, the ABCs Project could also be done among teachers and administrators for them to learn from one another before they apply the same process in their interactions with their students.

Instruction for Participants

For this project, you will complete the following:

- Write your autobiography to reflect on your family background, your learning experiences, and your vision.
- Work with other educators who are from a different cultural background than yours and get to know their backgrounds and their visions as educators.
- Write a biography of an educator you work with.
- Compare the autobiography and biography and identify any similarities and differences.
- Write a reflection to discuss what you learned from this experience and how you might apply what you learned to your teaching and your school.

Potential Challenges

As a comprehensive professional development activity, successful introduction and delivery of the ABCs Project requires the facilitator to build on educators' skills in learning about students, observing students, and directly interacting with the students and their families. We would recommend facilitators carefully consider sequencing the professional development activities in determining which version of the ABCs Project to use and when it best fits in your efforts to develop educators' critical cultural competence. Even though we provided instructions and handouts that could be used to facilitate the delivery of the activity, just like any other activities discussed in this book, without thoughtful implementation and purposeful reflection, participants will not be able to truly grow as critically culturally competent educators.

SUMMARY OF KEY POINTS

In this chapter, we provided several activities to further develop educators' critical cultural awareness and transformative actions to promote and lead changes in their local teaching contexts. Building on both agency and pathway thinking, we developed these activities to increase intercultural communication and offered different versions of the ABCs Projects that can be used in professional development to enhance educators' authentic practice.

- Serving as agents of change, educators with critical cultural competence are not content with only learning to use good teaching strategies. They challenge themselves to become better cultural brokers, are concerned about the cultural sensitivity development of themselves and others they work with, and are committed to initiating and leading changes and reforms at their schools and communities.
- Educators need to develop both agency and pathway thinking. With the goal to initiate transformative actions, they need to develop and maintain their motivation (agency thinking), and be willing to imagine the alternatives and innovative ways to achieve their goals (pathway thinking).
- Three specific activities are shared:
  - Activity 5.1 Active Listening
  - Activity 5.2 Classroom Observation Analysis
  - Activity 5.3 ABCs Project With Variations

REFLECTION AND EXTENSION

- Review activities introduced in previous chapters. How could you strategically combine and adapt various activities to design a series of professional development sessions for educators at your school or in your school district?

- What are the resources (experts, materials, community centers, etc.) in your local setting that are available to facilitate the preparation and delivery of activities introduced in this chapter?

ONLINE EXTENSIONS

These additional websites and online resources are recommended for learning more about cultural diversity for developing critical cultural competence:

- Geert Hofstede Cultural Dimensions Website (www.geert-hofst ede.com/). Hofstede studied the relationship between national cultures and organizational cultures, and identified five dimensions of culture through his large-scale studies: small versus large power distance, individualism versus collectivism, masculinity versus femininity, weak versus strong uncertainty avoidance, and long- versus short-term orientation. Each dimension offers insights into the impact of culture on communication patterns. The website presents a description of each dimension for major nations. Although there are criticisms to Hofstede's approach to studying cultural patterns, the information and resources from the website might help generate good discussions among educators regarding the impact of culture on cross-cultural communications.
- The Conflict Research Consortium at the University of Colorado offers online resources for active listening (www.colorado.edu/ conflict/peace/treatment/activel.htm). The website provides a brief overview of the concept and links to examples, approaches, and related problems. These resources might be helpful as the facilitator is preparing for this activity to build on educators' understanding of active listening strategies.
- For the observation analysis, the facilitator may want to consider introducing online tools such as Classroom Architect (http://classroom.4teachers.org/) that allow educators to outline classroom floor plans and use various drawing tools to note classrooms discourse patterns.

FOCUS FOR PROFESSIONAL LEARNING COMMUNITIES (PLCs)

All the activities introduced in this chapter require educators' authentic interactions with students and/or parents. If used in PLCs, the purposes of the PLCs' sessions would be to prepare educators for the activity and to share and debrief it. Both active listening and classroom observation analysis could be practiced in PLC sessions as a group; however, it is critical that educators actually start to apply the strategies and skills in their daily interactions with students, their families, and in the community. Even though it is beneficial for educators to complete an observation analysis based on videos of teaching, we would still highly recommend educators arrange to observe one another's classes and identify an authentic focus that is relevant to instruction. Among the activities introduced in Chapters 4 and 5, the ABCs Project is the most involved. If the PLC decides to focus on the ABCs Project, we would recommend the group plan for at least four to six sessions for the activity, as well as carefully plan and thoroughly discuss any challenges and cultural differences they may experience.

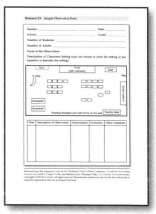

6

Learning About the Community

How Can We Learn More About Parents and Families?

Introduction

We all know that we are living in an era of standards-based reform. Fortunately, some of these reforms emphasize more deliberate engagement with the families and home communities of our students. In this chapter, we revisit the purpose of standards-based reforms, which are primarily intended as a mechanism for greater accountability. In response to such reforms, we describe methods for getting educators involved in the community based on Epstein's (1995, 2001) typology of traditional versus nontraditional ways of including and learning from parents. Most of these methods are being used in school systems across the United States with the goal of interacting with parents and families so teachers and administrators better understand how their students' home and neighborhood communities are the source of the worldviews that students bring to school each day. Additionally, community viewpoints inform us about how students understand teachers and administrators, the academic content with which they must engage, the relationships they create with peers and others, and how they interact with community members and others beyond their geographic locations. Therefore, the purpose of this chapter is to demonstrate how standards-driven instruction—coupled with knowledge about families and communities—can aid educators in becoming more critically culturally competent in their efforts to improve student achievement.

Standards-Based Reform

For more than 25 years, education has been guided by professional standards (Cochran-Smith & Fries, 2001; Delandshere & Petrosky, 2004). Such standards are supported by numerous educational and professional organizations: (1) the National Council for the Accreditation of Teacher Education (NCATE; n.d.), the accrediting body for colleges and universities that prepares teachers and other professional personnel for preschool through 12th-grade schools; (2) the Interstate New Teacher Assessment and Support Consortium (INTASC; 1992) standards, which stress "a common core of teaching knowledge and skills" (p. 6) that new teachers should know and be able to do; (3) the National Board of Professional Teaching Standards (NBPTS; n.d.), which highlights five core propositions that seek "to identify and recognize teachers who effectively enhance student learning and demonstrate a high level of knowledge, skills, abilities, and commitments" (p. 3); and (4) the Council for Exceptional Children (CEC; n.d.), which provides standards for the preparation and licensure of special education teachers. Further, content-area professional organizations, such as the National Council of Teachers of English (NCTE) and the National Council of Teachers of Mathematics (NCTM), to name just a few, also have standards related to teacher competence and pedagogical skill. These standards are designed to identify specific skills and competencies needed by teachers to move all students successfully through various levels of schooling and to ensure that high expectations will be maintained for students so they will perform at higher and more demanding levels.

To meet established standards, schools and teachers must guide students in their journey toward improved academic achievement. However, all involved parties—schools, communities, teachers, administrators, staff, parents, and students—have a personal and collective responsibility for the achievement of all students. As such, standards-based reforms demand that we must teach *all* students no matter what their diversity might be. For example, the 2001 No Child Left Behind federal legislation requires that test data in core content areas be disaggregated by "subcategories" such as race/ethnicity, socioeconomic status, gender, language/nationality, and exceptionality. If all target areas are met, then adequate yearly progress (AYP) is achieved. However, to be successful educators in this era of standards-based reform, expertise in the content area is only one requirement; the other requirement lies in the pedagogical skills needed to deliver the content to "everybody's children"—skills that those with only content-area knowledge or expertise may not consider, especially when the standards are designed by and for White, middle-class populations. Although assessment data is informative for designing and delivering instruction, overemphasis on testing results may blind us to skills some of our students bring into the classrooms. Therefore, teachers must show not only competence in their content areas and successful delivery of instruction that is effective but also evidence that they are constantly striving to improve their professional practice (Kozleski, Pugach, & Yinger, 2002). In addition, all educators need to know more about their students' backgrounds and how they learn.

Although each organization's standards acknowledge the need for content-area competence and pedagogical skills, they also explicitly cite the importance of parents, extended family, and community members, as well as partnerships and collaborations with community programs and agencies, as necessary components in the holistic education and schooling of all students. Further, given the reality of growing numbers of culturally and linguistically diverse students who are being taught overwhelmingly by monolingual, middle-class, White, female teachers in our schools today, it has become imperative for educators to intentionally seek out, recognize, and understand the strengths of the family and community as active and important partners in assuring that all students achieve at their highest possible levels (Kurtts, Ponder, & Cooper, 2006).

For example, NCATE (n.d.) unit standards try to ensure that the preparation of new teachers includes evidence of interactions with culturally diverse faculty and peers during a candidate's teacher education program. NCATE standards also mandate interactions with culturally diverse students, administrators, faculty, and staff in P–12 schools where candidates are completing their clinical experiences. INTASC Principle 10 directs us to "foster relationships with school colleagues, parents, and agencies in the larger community" (INTASC, 1992). Standards for accomplished teachers, set by the

NBPTS, require that "teachers work collaboratively with parents" and that they "take advantage of community resources" (NBPTS, n.d.). Explicitly recognizing that the families of students are culturally diverse and that these families may have different yet meaningful worldviews, Standard 10 of CEC's Performance-Based Standards calls for special education teachers to "routinely and effectively collaborate with families, other teachers, related service providers, and personnel from community agencies in culturally responsive ways" (CEC, n.d.). The Teaching of English to Speakers of Other Languages (TESOL; 2007) standards go a step further when they consider what affects the success of English Learners (ELs). In these standards, it is important for educators to understand and apply knowledge about cultural conflicts related to home events that have the potential to affect student learning. In addition, it is crucial for all educators to understand and apply knowledge about communication between home and school to intentionally improve their pedagogy and to build connections and partnerships with families of culturally and linguistically diverse students. Finally, it is vital to note that while the standards that include interactions with families and communities are designed to improve student achievement, they are also equally important for the development of educators' professional dispositions and exposure to cultures other than those with which they are already familiar.

Benefits of Involving Parents and Families in Schools

Our students' educational experiences actually begin in their homes and communities. From the time of their birth, children are immersed by their parents, guardians, extended families, and communities in environments where they are nurtured and raised until formal schooling begins. After all, according to Nicholas Hobbs (1978), parents are "the true experts on their children" (p. 496); in fact, "Parents are their children's first and most influential teachers" (Parents as Teachers, n.d.); they are vital contributors and equal partners in the education of their children (Johns, Crowley, & Guetzloe, 2001). Therefore, it would make sense that parents, and others who have initial interactions with their children, should partner with schools in providing the best educational experiences possible for them and in "caring for children we share" (Epstein, 1995, p. 701). More important, the shared interests that schools, parents, families, and communities have in children's educational development should encourage them to create better programs and opportunities for all students (Epstein, 1995). With this in mind, parental involvement (now, more commonly known as family involvement given the evolving compositions of families, which we will discuss further in Chapter 7) is federally mandated, and often, it is also state mandated (K. B. Grant & Ray, 2010). Federal legislation carried out by the U.S. Department of Education (2010), beginning with Title I of the Elementary and Secondary Education Act (ESEA) of 1965, a federal program created to meet the educational needs of children who experience low achievement in high-poverty schools up to the 2001 No Child Left Behind mandate, requires schools to partner with parents and families for improved student achievement. Further, the reauthorization of the ESEA continues to emphasize strengthening and supporting family engagement through programs and policies that engage and empower families. Moreover, families must have the information they need about how successful their children's schools and teachers are in educating their children, and administrators must consciously include families in the process of schooling their students (*Supporting Families and Communities: Reauthorizing the Elementary and Secondary Education Act*, n.d.).

The benefits of family involvement in children's education have been documented for some time now. In an extensive review and synthesis of research studies related to family involvement, Henderson and Mapp (2002) found that the benefits derived by students whose families were involved in their education included (1) higher grades and test scores; (2) higher rates of homework completion; (3) enrollment in higher-level classes, such as honors, advanced placement, and international baccalaureate courses; (4) promotion, passing classes, and earning college credits during high school; (5) attending school regularly; (6) demonstrating better social skills; (7) showing improved behavior; (8) having positive attitudes about and liking to go to school; and (9) graduating and moving to post-secondary education.

Additionally, there are benefits for parents, guardians, and community members as well. Through involvement with schools, parents, family members, and community members receive information about how they can assist their school-age children; they learn more about school and how the educational process progresses; they network with families of other students; and they gain further insights and have more positive views of teachers and school as a whole (Henderson & Mapp, 2002).

Traditional Ways of Involving Parents in Schools

Although there are various definitions of parent/family involvement (J. Smith & Wohlstetter, 2009), Joyce Epstein's (2001) developmental framework of six types of parent involvement is frequently used to analyze and guide parent involvement in schools. Her framework includes the integration of home, school, and community influences in children's learning and development. Though this six-part typology has been criticized as being "too school-based and Eurocentric" (J. Smith & Wohlstetter, 2009, p. 5), Epstein (1995) suggests that parents can participate in their children's education in various ways.

Figure 6.1 Epstein's Framework of Six Types of Involvement

Type	Description
Type 1—Parenting	Help all families establish home environments to support children as students
Type 2—Communicating	Design effective forms of school-to-home and home-to-school communications about school programs and children's progress
Type 3—Volunteering	Recruit and organize parent help and support
Type 4—Learning at Home	Provide information and ideas to families about how to help students at home with homework and other curriculum-related activities, decisions, and planning
Type 5—Decision Making	Include parents in school decisions, developing parent leaders and representatives
Type 6—Collaborating With Community	Identify and integrate resources and services from the community to strengthen school programs, family practices, and student learning and development

Source: Epstein, 1995, p. 704.

Type 1 focuses on parents (and families) readying children to learn by keeping them safe and healthy. Parents and family members teach children respect for their roles as parents as well as positive beliefs and values. Children are also taught by their parents the importance and responsibilities of their attendance in school and develop confidence in their abilities to succeed in school. Traditional home–school activities that fall in this category include school- and community-based workshops and computerized phone messages on parenting and child rearing for different ages and grade levels. Home visits for sharing ways to help children learn and be ready for school and neighborhood meetings are also included in Type 1 activities. Additionally, parenting skills can be enhanced through parent education courses provided by the school.

Type 2 activities involve various communications about children's progress in schools. For example, schools have open houses at the beginning of the academic year so parents can meet the teachers of their children. Now, academic requirements and behavioral expectations for classes are shared orally and in writing. School handbooks are disseminated so school policies and procedures can be made public and accessible to the entire school's population. Throughout the school year, folders containing weekly homework, graded assignments, and class newsletters are sent home to communicate students' progress. Parents are invited again to the school to personally pick up the first report card of the school year where a conference can be held if requested. Other meetings are scheduled to assist students and their families in students' transitioning from grade level to grade level (i.e., transitioning from middle school to high school or from high school to college).

Type 3 practices involve volunteerism. Schools welcome volunteers to assist with a variety of tasks, such as office assistance, sports events, parent–teacher association (PTA) membership recruitment, book fairs, open houses, PTA events, grade mothers/fathers, school performances, chaperones on field trips, reading aloud to students, tutoring, and the like. Some schools send correspondence to ascertain particular talents of parents and family members. For example, school personnel may seek parents who have journalistic or technology skills so a school newsletter can be generated or a website maintained. In addition, various communications recruiting parents and family members as volunteers are shared throughout the school year.

Type 4 activities entail parents becoming involved in supporting the actual schoolwork of children in the home environment. Information is disseminated giving parents information on how they can help their children with both homework and extracurricular activities. Material about homework policies and how to monitor homework are shared as well. Additionally, schools can keep parents informed through calendars that include school and class activities and upcoming events and assignments. Family math, science, and literacy activities are held at the school to help parents become more involved with and knowledgeable about their children's academic progression. Summer learning material is sent home so parents can sustain their children's learning experiences from the previous school year and help them prepare for the upcoming academic year. Additionally, families are invited to pro-vide insight, along with teachers, to students when they begin setting their goals for postsecondary education and/or the world of work.

Type 5 practices encourage avenues for parents' voices to contrib-ute to school policies and procedures that affect their children's educa-tion. Including their voice in school governance issues allows parents to feel a sense of ownership of the school, not only as an educational institution that serves their children but also as a community organiza-tion that prepares informed citizens for a democratic society. Parents also become aware of school, district, and state policies. In other words, parents also become leaders in providing educational opportunities and programming for their children.

Finally, Type 6 activities invite the collaboration of parents with the community. Recognizing that positive child and adolescent develop-ment extends beyond the academic environment, schools help fami-lies become more involved in their children's education by identifying community resources and services that could assist in the physical, mental, emotional, and psychological well-being of their children. Information on various community agencies (i.e., health centers, den-tal clinics, mental health centers, recreation centers) is shared with families. Summer enrichment materials and other community activi-ties that can enhance the development of children and adolescents are also provided for families. Service activities by both students and families (i.e., working with senior citizens, recycling) also demonstrate collaboration with the community.

In summary, all six types of parent/family involvement as delin-eated by Epstein (2001) represent ways that are mutually beneficial to parents and to school personnel. Activities within any one of the six types encourage partnerships with schools, families, and communi-ties for helping students become all they can be. Further, any of these activities can provide avenues with which teachers and administra-tors can learn more about families and community members of their students.

Nontraditional Approaches to Parents and Involvement

Though Epstein's (1995, 2001) six-part typology of parental involve-ment has been widely used, given the composition and needs of today's families, nontraditional ways of parent/family involvement must be considered, too. Moll and Greenberg (1990) described the use of funds of knowledge, rich repositories of knowledge found in children's homes and communities. Households are educational settings where knowledge, skills, and dispositions are transmitted from one generation to another. Additionally, households are the source of social histories; methods of thinking, doing, and learning; and practical skills (Genzuk, 1999) related to work and play that, if used sincerely and intentionally and without a deficit perspective, can be instructive and quite useful in curriculum integration.

As an example, Arias and Morillo-Campbell (2008) compare traditional and nontraditional approaches to EL parental involvement that can be used for all families. Instead of assisting parents with parenting skills, which is a more school-centered, traditional approach to parental involvement, a different goal is to develop "reciprocal understandings" (p. 13) of the purpose of schools and schooling and for parents to be able to advance themselves (e.g., their literacy development) through how and what their children are learning at school. Although communication with families about what is going on academically and socially with their children and in the school as a whole is very important, taking a different approach would "situate cultural strengths of family and community within the school curriculum" (p. 13). Further, parental advocacy education could inform and teach parents and families how to effectively and confidently advocate for the needs of their children. By learning about how to advocate for their children, parents can feel empowered through efforts they initiate themselves at school and in the community level. Finally, this advocacy could lead to including culturally and linguistically appropriate practices in every aspect of schooling experiences to maximizing learning opportunities for the entire community.

Barriers and Facilitators to Involvement

Even with various traditional activities of parent and family involvement being encouraged by standards-based reform, barriers to schools, parents, families, and communities partnering with one another continue. School-based barriers include the persistence of deficit perspectives and beliefs about diverse populations (Arias & Morillo-Campbell, 2008). Some educators consider culturally and linguistically diverse students and their families deficient because they may not be as fluent in Standard English and are, therefore, considered a "problem" in communication. Culturally and linguistically diverse families are frequently perceived as lacking resources—knowledge, skills, and experiences— necessary for their children to succeed in schools. Differences in cultural expectations of how schools are viewed have also led to misunderstandings about expectations for parental/family involvement in schools. Parents may be quite interested in their children's education even if they do not participate in traditional ways that schools find acceptable. For example, some parents' schedules do not allow them to come to school during the day to volunteer or to attend school conferences or meetings at night, such as the PTA meeting. Also, some parents are not as well versed in the academic content their children are learning to be of great assistance to them. As a result, when homework is not completed, teachers become frustrated and blame families for not caring for and about their children.

There are ways to address these barriers, however. Communication with parents, families, and communities can be improved and promoted by providing home–school coordinators or liaisons to serve as information sources between schools and the families. Of course, home visits by educators are advocated, but when home visits are not possible, a community visit could provide teachers and administrators with great insights in helping make lessons and social relations with students and families more culturally relevant. Bilingual newsletters and multilingual telephone homework lines are most inviting for families, and will permit them to be informed about and involved in their children's progress, even if they do not understand English. Such actions are public acknowledgment that schools recognize and appreciate the cultural values of all families. Furthermore, instead of having parents come to school for meetings, schools can schedule meetings in the community. After all, strengths are found in communities, too, and these strengths can be incorporated into the curriculum. Scheduling meetings to accommodate families' work schedules and providing child care at such meetings could engender more attendance and participation. Given the particular needs of the community, schools could also arrange for transportation for students who are engaged in after-school activities (Arias & Morillo-Campbell, 2008).

Extending Traditional Approaches to Parent and Family Involvement

Thus far, we have described how parental/family involvement is supported by the standards that schools and teachers are accountable for. Our hope is that teachers and administrators will move beyond following only traditional activities for teacher–parent–community interaction to maximize opportunities for parental and family involvement.

Later, we provide a slightly different take on three activities that can move educators beyond their classrooms and schools into the home communities of their learners. Considered traditional activities by some, if done correctly and without a deficit lens, we believe they can be powerful ways to connect with parents and families.

ACTIVITY 6.1 TOURING THE NEIGHBORHOOD—THE DO'S AND DON'TS

In an effort to be sensitive to the plights of all children who enter our nation's schools, school administrations may offer or require either bus tours or walking tours of the neighborhoods of their students and families to their teachers and other staff. Since poverty has been cited as a cause of low achievement (Lee, 2002), many administrators across the country want their staff to see the low-income neighborhoods that feed into their schools. There are two ways to view this activity. On one hand, seeing neighborhoods where children play and live can give teachers and other school personnel a vision of where children go when they are not in school. Some might say that knowing where the neighborhood is and what it comprises would spark more culturally rich teaching experiences for the students. On the other hand, this activity could be perceived as deficit laden. Loading educators on a bus or taking them on a walking tour of low-income neighborhood can be likened to a Hollywood actor's home tour without the glamour. While sightseers tour Hollywood neighborhoods commenting on the opulence of lifestyles and wishing that they could experience such living, being on a tour of low-income neighborhoods oftentimes may result in silent fear, disdain, and/or pity. Such tours may only reinforce preconceived beliefs held by many educators that these parents do not care for themselves; thus, they do not care for or about their children. Questions may be raised such as "I work. Why don't they work?" "Why don't they get jobs?" "People just want to live off welfare." Moreover, if teachers and administrators remain as "visitors" peering into communities, such actions give members of the community the impression that they are not worthy to be touched or heard. These neighborhood folks have voices and stories to tell. Perhaps, it is time to *get off the bus* and talk *with*, not to, these citizens about the ways they view the world. After all, they are the experts of their lived experiences. The information gleaned from them could potentially aid administrators, teachers, and other school personnel in understanding more about how students come to believe, perceive, and receive school and the actions that occur in it. Further, getting off the bus to interact with community members can, hopefully, debunk some of the preconceived stereotypes the sightseers had in the first place. Students from the neighborhood, who may be resistant in some classes, may shift their perceptions of their teachers and their school through such interactions as well.

(Continued)

(Continued)

Objectives

- To interact with people living in the local community
- To get to know community members, their beliefs, their values, and their perceptions of schools
- To learn the strengths of communities
- To become familiar with students' home communities in an effort to make instruction more culturally responsive

Suggestions/Backgrounds for Facilitation

In planning and executing a neighborhood bus tour, several steps are recommended. They are as follows:

- It is respectful to the neighborhood's inhabitants, especially if it is a public housing neighborhood, to let the manager know of your plan to visit. In fact, knowledge of the visit should be made well in advance. Managers may provide useful advice, and may offer to speak to people on the bus. Questions can be asked and answered; however, this action does not take the place of getting off the bus and interacting with others. It is also very important that school personnel seek knowledge from the neighborhood's inhabitants and not appear to "know it all." If they do, they defeat the purpose of the visit. School personnel are seeking to know how parents, families, and community members can become partners with them in helping all students succeed in school.
- Prepare the school staff for the tour with information on percentages of students who reside in the neighborhood, the neighborhood's history (how it came to be), and the names of the schools from which the neighborhood children are bused. In preparation, be sure to speak to systemic and institutional reasons for the existence of the neighborhood. Why was the neighborhood built in the first place? Why was it built in this particular location?
- Once arrangements are made, ask staff members to interrogate their beliefs about what they will see and how they feel about the children from these neighborhoods and their capacities to learn. Ask them how they feel about the students' parents and why they feel the way they do. This exercise may be done silently without any answers expected. Nevertheless, the questions must be asked!

Instructions to Participants

When the tour actually occurs, sightseers must get off the bus and speak with people in the community. Depending on when the tour takes place, seek to speak to as many parents, grandparents, and other community members as possible.

Make sure that teachers and administrators reveal who they are, why they are visiting, and that they seek to find out about the neighborhood's strengths. Perhaps a calendar of school events could be shared with everyone as a gift and as an invitation to become a more vital member of the school's family.

Exhibiting fear is a definite don't! Believe it or not, the neighbors will know it, and they will surmise that your visit is not genuine.

On returning to school, reflect on the visit and process with others what you learned and unlearned.

Recommended Questions Following the Activity (I=Individual Reflection Questions, G=Group Discussion Questions)

- How did you feel about taking the tour before it occurred? What apprehensions, if any, did you have (I, G)?
- What caused you to have the feelings that you did? Were there previous events in your life that led you to feel the way you did? (I, G)
- How did you feel when you stepped off the bus? (I, G)
- What did it feel like to walk through the neighborhood and speak with people? (I, G)
- What surprised you most? Why? (I, G)
- What will you do with what you learned? How will this activity inform your instruction and relationships with your students and their families? (I, G)
- Will you do this activity again? Why? If so, what would you do differently? (I, G)

Time

- This activity takes two hours or more depending on how many communities the teachers, staff, and administrators will visit and on how much time will be spent with the neighborhood inhabitants in each community.

ACTIVITY 6.2 HOME VISITS AT THE BEGINNING OF THE SCHOOL YEAR

Home visits are a time-honored tradition in schools, especially in the elementary grades. Usually completed at the beginning of the school year, home visits tend to take place in homes of low-income families. The central purpose of these visits is to build trust and respect between teachers and families and to inform parents of their children's academic progress. Schools, for some, lack credibility among parents because of prior experiences that parents have had there. In essence, some parents' prior feelings—positive or negative—about school are reenacted

(Continued)

(Continued)

through their children's experiences. Thus, some parents do not have positive feelings about school.

However, home visits can assist educators in becoming aware of students' cultural backgrounds as lived in their home communities. In other words, teachers and administrators benefit because they can increase their cultural competence and knowledge base about where families come from. Initially, home visits were designed to "end the cycle of blame at schools with histories of low student achievement" (The Parent Teacher Home Visit Project, 2011, para. 1). These visits explicitly demonstrate and value that parents are partners with schools in providing a meaningful education for their children. In addition, home visits also reflect the shared responsibility that school personnel and parents have for their children's continued academic achievement. This genuine display of caring can open or increase lines of communication with families; it is by no means used for assessments and interventions (The Parent Teacher Home Visit Project, 2011). Instead, it is a time for dreams, hopes, and aspirations about the "children we share" to be communicated.

Home visits by educators change the school as a location of the "culture of power" (Delpit, 2010). The school building itself represents the halls of power. Moreover, schools represent institutions filled with knowledgeable people who make decisions about the futures of children. For some parents, teachers and other school personnel are omniscient. By visiting homes, educators greet parents in environments where children's educational beginnings occurred. Furthermore, educators are going to parents instead of parents coming to them. They are going to the first expert on their students' lives—their parents. Making such an effort is always important in creating partnerships for the betterment of children.

Objectives

- To visit homes and get to know parents, guardians, and other family members
- To learn from parents, guardians, and other family members of their expectations and hopes for their children
- To share school expectations and identify best ways for communication

Instructions to Participants

When making home visits, it is important to remember the following:

- Always preschedule home visits. There is nothing worse than to show up unannounced. Further, depending on individual students, they may want to be present during the visit. If trust is an issue, it would be wise to include the student in the visit. For some students, it is important for them to hear what teachers or administrators say about them.

- It is most important that educators honor the cultures of the homes they are visiting. Before the visit, it would be great if they spoke with individual students about what might be expected in the visit. For example, do some parents require that shoes be removed when entering the home? Is it customary to eat whatever is offered? Is it offensive to say, "No, thank you?" Finding out what proper etiquette is also a demonstration of the time and effort you are making to assure the success of the home visit.

- Some parents may not want to meet teachers or administrators in their homes. If this is the case, choose a mutually agreed on location, preferably one that the parent chooses.

- Unless you know the community well, safety issues must be considered. This caution is not to say that all neighborhoods are dangerous places to visit. However, it is a good idea when visiting anywhere to inform others of your whereabouts. Carry a cell phone in case you get lost, and pair with another colleague and make the visits together. Daytime visits are preferred; nonetheless, choose a time that is agreed on by both parties.

- It is most important that educators begin the conversation with how honored they are to be working with the parents' children. Parents don't want to begin a conversation with how difficult their child is and the problems the child is creating. Begin conversations positively.

- It is also vital that teachers and administrators share information about themselves. By doing so, parents can see them as human and fallible. Such sharing invites the discovery of commonalities between parents and educators. In addition, sharing information that can be left with families is always a good gesture. You might leave study materials for families to assist children in their learning.

- Think about where you are and how you would feel if you were being visited by a teacher or administrator. In other words, choose your words and actions carefully. A home visit should be a positive, instructive experience for all involved.

- Not all students require a home visit each year. It depends on the grade level and the school. For instance, in the lower grades, visiting each home of kindergarteners is quite appropriate. It may be somewhat more difficult in sixth grade where there are more students per teacher. We realize that some teachers may want to be "fair" and visit *all* students in their classes. Nevertheless, some students need the visit more than others. Careful selection of who needs the visit should not be driven by fear, but by need on both parts—the students, the teachers, and the administrators. Some educators need to visit certain communities to dismantle prior beliefs about them. Others may need to visit communities in an effort to make their instruction more culturally responsive and to inform themselves who their students are and where they are educated outside of school.

(Continued)

(Continued)

- When home visits are not possible, another possibility for seeing students outside the walls of school is community visits. Sometimes, students who may not excel in school show competence in other areas of their lives. Some of them sing, dance, and play organized sports in their communities. We recommend that for some students, especially those who appear disengaged in school, a community visit is quite appropriate. Visiting a community center football or basketball game to watch particular students sends a positive message to students, their families, and their community members that their teachers or administrators are willing to go an extra mile to see students achieve. Educators who make this effort will be pleasantly surprised at the community's response to their presence. Additionally, they should notice the difference in attitudes and behaviors of the students they visited.

Recommended Questions Following the Activity (I=Individual Reflection Questions, G=Group Discussion Questions)

- Was the request for a home visit your idea or was it the mandate of your administrator? (I, G)
- What were your thoughts about making the visits? What, if any, were your apprehensions? Did you have to visit all the students or select students? (I, G)
- How did you prepare for the visit? Did you prepare materials to share with families? (I, G)
- Did you need an interpreter? Was one provided? (I, G)
- Did your nonverbal behavior complement your conversation? Believe it not, people can tell when others are uncomfortable around them or want to make hurried visits. (I, G)
- How were you received during the home visit? How did you think the home visit went? (I, G)
- How did you feel after the visit occurred? Were any of your preconceived beliefs confirmed? Explain. (I. G)
- What were the strengths you found in the home? In the community? (I, G)
- Would you make home visits on your own or would you initiate the visits themselves even if they had to occur after school began? What would you do differently from what you did in previous home visits? (I, G)

Time

- Time needed for this activity will depend on the distance needed to travel to the home and the time needed to speak with parents. However, the actual visit should take no more than 30 minutes to 1 hour. Parents could be guides in determining how long the visit should take. Additionally, time should be allotted for debriefing visits among colleagues.

ACTIVITY 6.3 PREPARING FOR
THE FIRST PARENT CONFERENCE

Parent conferences can be a valuable strategy for improving classroom academic performance and student behavior. Such meetings can be another vehicle through which parents and teachers can communicate. Although there are various websites that offer information on how to hold successful parent conferences, in an effort to receive maximum benefit from parent conferences, the following considerations should be made.

Objectives

- To meet parents of students
- To assure parents of the school–home partnership that teachers, administrators, and parents share
- To provide information about students' academic progress
- To seek advice from parents on how students' educational experiences can be maximized

Instructions to Participants

Make sure the purpose of the conference is clear to all those concerned. What do you want to share with parents? Whatever information is being shared, begin with something positive about the student. Similar to home visits, a parent conference should not begin with a complaint. Remember, parents are sending to school what they consider extensions of themselves, and parents more often than not want more for their children than what they had for themselves.

Teachers and administrators alike should interrogate themselves about the issues that are being presented. Is the conference being held as a means of removing the student from class because of an implicit reason that is not being shared? Is the conference being held because the student has taken power or control from you because you allowed it? Be concise, yet definitive about your concerns. Sometimes parent conferences are moments to affirm the student's progress. Other times, these meetings serve to express concern about academic difficulty and behavioral issues. Those concerns should be expressed in a way that shows how one impacts the other. Let parents know that you care about what happens to their child and that you need their assistance to alleviate the concern.

Documentation of behaviors is a *must*! This documentation should be specific with notations of dates, times, actions, names of others involved, and responses to behaviors by all parties concerned.

(Continued)

(Continued)

As in home visits, conferences must be made at the parents' convenience. The culture of power at school is reinforced more when teachers or administrators are not flexible with times they can meet with parents. By accommodating parents' schedules, educators send the message they are willing to do whatever is necessary to help the child succeed.

Allow the parent or family member to be the expert regarding the child's home experiences. In fact, it would not be a bad idea to include a time during the conference when parents/family members can share what they know about their child. This sharing explicitly positions the parent in being a copartner in educating their child. The power position is minimized, but no less important. In other words, this action levels the playing field.

Recognize and honor cultural differences that might be expressed during the conference. Those differences may include referring to parents by name. Some cultures prefer to be called by their titles—Mr. or Mrs.—and not by their first names. Only call parents by their first name if they give you permission to do so. Another difference might be ways that parents are involved with their children. Assumptions are often made by school personnel that parents are not involved with their children's education *in ways teachers believe are appropriate* when in actuality parents are very involved in their children's learning *according to definitions in their cultures*. Finally, because educators may not be familiar with family and community meanings and frames of reference that children bring with them to school, children's ways of understanding and acting, such as verbal responses and behaviors, may often be misunderstood, thus, misinterpreted. Instead of blaming the student during the conference, ask the parents about these behaviors to ascertain their actual meanings.

Inquire about special talents that students have. While school may not be a favorite place for some students, other places outside school may be venues where their competence is demonstrated. Such knowledge by educators could inform them of culturally responsive ways of reaching these students. Furthermore, educators then have the opportunity of learning about their students in different environments to which they would not otherwise be privy.

Remember that teachers and administrators are not diagnosticians! Most of them do not have professional licenses to diagnose such conditions as attention deficit hyperactivity disorder. Furthermore, because we do not live in our students' households, we should not attempt to determine what goes on there without actual knowledge of it.

Conferences are private matters between the parents and their child's teacher. Discussions occurring within them should not be shared with others, unless the information is beneficial to others who teach the student. To be on the safe side, always ask the parent if it is permissible to share information with others who are involved with the student.

Recommended Questions Following the Activity (I=Individual Reflection Questions, G=Group Discussion Questions)

- What were your initial thoughts about conducting the parent conference? Did preconceived notions or prior communication about the child influence your thoughts? (I, G)
- Were you clear about the purpose of the conference? Was it about an academic issue, a behavioral issue, or both? (I)
- How did you begin the conference? Do you think the parents felt like a contributor to their child's educational process? (I)
- In speaking with the parent(s), did you do most of the talking or did you allow the parent to inform you about the child? Why or why not? (I, G)
- In what ways could you use the information that the parent(s) shared to assist you in helping the child? (I, G)
- Did you establish a means of communicating with the parent(s) about the child's progress? If so, how? (I, G)
- How do you think the parent conference went? How do you think the parent(s) thought about the conference? (I, G)
- What did you learn about yourself as you conducted the conference? What could you do to improve conducting a parent conference? (I, G)

SUMMARY OF KEY POINTS

This chapter provided an overview of how standards-based reform has been a catalyst for the intentional inclusion of parent, family, and community engagement as an important part of the work of teachers, administrators, and schools. Many professional organizations have emphasized the importance of families and communities as our students' first teachers; therefore, it is important that relationships are fostered among educators, parents/families, communities, and schools as partners in educating all children. We discussed traditional activities for getting to know and involving parents and families in schools by reviewing Joyce Epstein's (1995) framework for parent/family involvement. We also shared barriers and facilitators to parent involvement as well as some nontraditional ways that parents can be involved in their children's education. Finally, we offered three activities to involve parents in their children's education that, although considered traditional by some, work best when teachers and administrators leave their schools to enter and learn from the home communities of their learners.

- Activity 6.1 Touring the Neighborhood—The Do's and Don'ts
- Activity 6.2 Home Visits at the Beginning of the School Year
- Activity 6.3 Preparing for the First Parent Conference

REFLECTION AND EXTENSION

- Choose one of the three activities described previously to do yourself, using it to share aspects of your personal cultural identity and how you may appear to parents, families, and other community members of your students.
- What are some other activities or questions you use to help educators better understand themselves as cultural beings when they visit the communities of their learners?
- How can you adapt some of your favorite activities that involve parents to make teaching more culturally responsive for your students?

ONLINE EXTENSIONS

The purpose of these activities is for educators to leave their school to enter homes and communities where their students are also educated. Physically entering the communities is vital as educators make a conscious, committed effort to go to parents and families instead of them coming to the school. Therefore, we do not offer online extensions to these activities. Even if the other activities are completed via online connections, we recommend that the neighborhood bus tour, home visit, and parent conference actually be done face-to-face. While the parent conference can take place by telephone, we advise that person-to-person contact be made. However, reflections and discussions following these activities can be completed in online environments.

FOCUS FOR PROFESSIONAL LEARNING COMMUNITIES (PLCs)

The activities for learning more about parents, families, and communities described in this chapter are ideal for PLCs to undertake. Even if the school's leadership does not require home visits or neighborhood walking or bus tours, PLCs could make this one of their goals at the start of each year. The information learned can be foundational to planning future goals for the PLC, and it can provide additional data to be evaluated in helping improve the academic achievement of students. Each of the activities in this chapter, whether undertaken in a traditional or nontraditional way, is not meant to be done alone. Touring the neighborhood and making home visits are best done in groups, and certainly, discussing and debriefing what educators learn about their students' parents, families, and communities from these experiences is also best done in groups. This is why we say that these activities are ideal for PLCs. Even discussing the results of parent conferences in PLC sessions is valuable because what one teacher or administrator learns and shares may help the group in making better decisions about how to work with students and how to focus the work of the PLC. Also, because many educators are already using Epstein's Framework of Six Types of Involvement in their school, PLCs should brainstorm new ideas to communicate and partner with parents beyond classroom settings—without a deficit lens and with their school's particular context and their students' communities in mind—to build stronger, more personal connections with parents, families, and other community members.

7

Community-Based Learning

How Can We Learn From Parents, Families, and Communities?

Introduction

In this chapter, we discuss the importance of families and communities as key influences in the socialization and development of their children—especially their educational development. Additionally, we convey the importance of partnering with families and communities to provide the best education for children, which is vital in every child's P–12 educational journey. We know that our classrooms and schools mirror our increasingly diverse society because school attendance is compulsory for American youth—at least to age 16. However, we may not always realize that along with their physical presence, students also bring their individual and collective multiple identities, values, beliefs, traditions, ways of knowing, and ways of doing to our schools. And with each student who comes into our schools, the foundations of their worldviews—their families and communities—also enter our classrooms.

How diverse are families and our communities?

Although culturally diverse families—those who are ethnically and linguistically diverse, as well as those with different socioeconomic and religious backgrounds—are visible to educators, we should not forget that other family demographics influence how children's worldviews are shaped. For instance, the two-parent, nuclear family is no longer dominant. Single-parent families and blended families are growing in number (K. B. Grant & Ray, 2010; James, 2009). Also, a growing number of grandparents are primary caregivers for their grandchildren (Fuller-Thomson & Minkler, 2001). In addition, same-sex families and adoptive families are rising (Gajda, 2004; Gelnaw, Brickley, Marsh, & Ryan, 2004; Gilmore & Bell, 2006). Finally, because of national and international affairs, more children are entering our schools from families in transition because of their immigrant or refugee status. We also have children who might have experienced the death of a parent, have a parent in the military, have a parent in prison, or live with foster parents. No matter what the family demographics may be, the ways in which families are perceived by teachers, administrators, and other school personnel can influence how children are motivated to achieve. Furthermore, how engaged their parents, guardians, or extended family members are in the schooling of their children is known to influence academic achievement (Epstein, 1995, 2001; Hill & Craft, 2003).

Partnering With Parents, Families, and Communities

We also know that parents/guardians and extended family members are our children's first teachers. From the time of birth, children acquire skills related to certain ways of comprehending and problem solving in their homes and communities. Homes and communities play vital roles in how cultures are created, learned, and practiced by our children as they grow (Vygotsky, 1978). It is in the home community that "standards for deciding what is, standards for deciding what can be, standards for deciding how one feels about it, standards for deciding what to do about it, and standards for deciding how to go about doing it" (Goodenough, 1963, pp. 258–259) are grounded. Therefore, to value the diversity of whom children are and where they come from, educators must recognize that parents/guardians and other family members are the first teachers in children's lives. With firsthand knowledge of our students' family values and "standards," teachers and administrators can learn ways to deliver academic content more effectively so each student can learn. However, we cannot desire partnerships with parents without also considering associations and linkages with their home communities. In other words, school personnel need to be cognizant of skills and understandings that children bring to school from their communities to make the connection between students' backgrounds and the diverse ways they comprehend and problem solve at school.

As discussed in Chapter 6, the need to acknowledge and involve parents in their children's education has been recognized in school reform and included in restructuring efforts for many years (Epstein & Sanders, 2006). In fact, we have empirical evidence that parental/family involvement enhances the quality of the educational experience for students, including their achievement (Gordon & Louis, 2009; Hawes & Plourde, 2005; Hong & Ho, 2005; Jeynes, 2007; Simon, 2001). Therefore, we clearly know the benefits of parental/family/community involvement in the lives of school-age children. Nonetheless, as we work to effectively meet the needs of 21st-century learners, we must design more meaningful instruction and professional development for teachers and administrators that creates interactive ways for families and communities to be even more valued and involved in the schooling of their children. One way of doing so is engaging educators in community-based learning that goes beyond the physical structure of the classroom and the school. The home communities of our students offer a wealth of knowledge that has yet to be tapped by teachers and administrators and integrated into our school settings (Owens & Wang, 1996).

What is community-based learning?

Community-based learning is as an action-oriented method to help educators learn more about other cultures, especially the home communities of their students. This pedagogical strategy not only links theory to practice but also allows educators to immerse themselves in cultures different from theirs (Boyle-Baise, 2005; Boyle-Baise & Sleeter, 1998; Burant & Kirby, 2002; Carter, Cadge, Rivero, & Curran, 2002; Cooper, 2007; Mooney & Edwards, 2001; Owens & Wang, 1996; Sleeter, 2000, 2001).

Cultural immersion experiences, a form of community-based learning, are valuable for all educators, but especially for those who work in urban environments. Such experiential learning opportunities afford teachers and administrators chances to learn from the communities that they serve. In fact, community teacher knowledge (Murrell, 2001) allows educators "to view, experience, reflect upon, and change perspectives of how others respond to and make sense of their worlds" (Cooper, 2007, p. 264). More important, community-based learning acknowledges that "intelligence and expertise are built out of interaction with the environment, not in isolation from it" and that "effective learning engages both head and hand and requires both knowing and doing" (Owens & Wang, 1996, p. 6). When educators actively seek to gain knowledge from their learners' home communities, and when they really understand the daily experiences of their learners' families, this makes a public declaration that parents/guardians, families, and community members are extremely important in the education of all children.

Such knowledge is best gained through community-based learning activities. These activities can be done in a day or can be completed through prolonged engagement in the communities of our students and their families. Whatever the period for completion, the following considerations are key. First, activities must have pedagogical components, including specific goals, which must be directly linked to educators' classroom and school practices. Second, learning activities must not be viewed as those in which educators view themselves as "saviors to the lost." Each culture has understandings that are central to survival and acceptance in that particular culture. In other words, what may not make sense to us may be quite comprehensible and acceptable in the culture in which we are temporarily members. Third, the ideal community-based activity should be designed in partnership with members of the community, agency, culture, and so on that educators will visit and learn. Authenticity of engagement is crucial. Thus, detailed planning that is shared with others in the community is important to assure the credibility and the amplification of the community's voice. Fourth, as we have been emphasizing throughout this book, participant reflection with guided questions is a must. It is not enough for educators to provide a summary of their experiences. Thought-provoking, challenging questions must be asked that will allow for critical examination of what was observed and how participants felt before, during, and after the community engagement occurred. In sum, community-based activities must be mutually beneficial to the educator as well as to the community.

Community-Based Learning Activities

What follows is a description of two activities we have used for several years that help both inexperienced and experienced teachers take their first steps into learning more about the communities in which their students reside. The overarching goal of these community-based activities is to better understand the lived experiences of students and to make good use of what they learn from these experiences in their teaching and other interactions at school. We call these two community-based learning opportunities the Home–Community Camera Adventure and Walking a Mile in Another's Shoes. We describe the goals for these activities as well as details for how to prepare participants to complete them and reflect on their learning. We also provide examples of the kinds of learning that teachers have expressed to us because of engaging in these community-based adventures. Although these activities initially involved teachers, all school personnel can benefit from doing these community-based activities.

ACTIVITY 7.1 HOME-COMMUNITY CAMERA ADVENTURE

Objectives

- To help educators learn about their students' lives in the communities where they live with their families
- To undermine stereotypical beliefs about *all* people who live in a particular neighborhood
- To learn to access members of the community to answer questions
- To gain knowledge, skills, and dispositions to take back to schools by having overcome fears about what had previously appeared to be unknown

Planning and Preparation

One strategy for finding which home communities to visit is to meet with school personnel responsible for keeping records about school bus routes or to ask the principal, social worker, or home–school coordinator. Before the actual visit, the following should occur:

- The educator should select a student with whom he or she has been working to explore the student's community. Educators can also cull the list of school-feeder communities that bus children into their school to help them

(Continued)

(Continued)

select a student. In some cases, the student's community might be a public-housing area, an ethnic minority community, and/or a linguistically diverse community. In any case, it is important to note that the community chosen must be ethnically/culturally/linguistically different from the educator's background. In other words, an African American educator should not complete this activity in an African American community.

- The appropriate authorities must give clearance regarding choices of neighborhoods and communities to visit. Moreover, if educators are visiting public-housing communities, we recommend asking formal permission from the housing-community manager after thoroughly explaining the goals of this activity. Candidly, housing managers are usually very happy that school personnel are willing to seek out and learn about the strengths of the community. Nonetheless, there have been times when educators were not welcome into some communities. Such situations were remedied by choosing other communities.

- Communities should be visited during daytime hours. Inservice teachers, in particular, need to be provided coverage to complete this activity, unless they prefer to do it after school or on a weekend. In the past, some teachers have sought parental permission so their student could actually accompany the teachers on the Camera Adventure. It is amazing to see how students value their community and how they can help school personnel see what is important to them. Educators can always complete the Home-Community Camera Adventure successfully in small groups, so pairing educators in groups of two or three to visit communities is best.

Photo by Melissa Madison.

Instruction to Participants

During the home-community visit, at least one member of the group should have a camera. However, it is better when all educators have cameras and take pictures from their own perspectives while still following the guidelines provided for the Camera Adventure. Educators should take pictures of whatever they experience. However, with each person taking at minimum of 10 photographs, pictures should be taken based on the following:

- Something historic of which you were not aware
- Something that shows the natural beauty of the area
- A scenic or panoramic view
- Something that shows the area is changing
- Something that shows the resources available in this community
- Something that could be used in a tourism brochure to advertise this part of the school community to entice people to come to the home community
- Something that shows growth in the area
- Something that is kid-friendly
- Something that you or your group feels could be improved about the area
- Something that surprised you or your group about the area
- Other scenes that you find interesting and want to add to this project

Recommended Questions Following the Activity (I=Individual Reflection Questions, G=Group Discussion Questions)

After photographs are taken, each educator answers reflective questions about Home-Community Camera Adventure including writing about how they perceived it, what dispositions they felt while doing it, and how they would use what they learned in their classrooms. Reflection questions included the following:

- When this activity was first described, how did you feel? Were you apprehensive about going into the community? (I, G)
- How did you acquire information about the community before going to it? (I, G)
- Was the community what you expected it to be? (I, G)
- What shocked you most? (I, G)
- What did you learn professionally from this activity? (I, G)
- What did you learn about yourself personally from this activity?
- How do you think this experience will affect your actual teaching?
- Would you do the experience again? Why or why not?

Educators should also share their findings and their new insights with others. This can be done in several ways, although we have had great success with different formats for sharing results of the Home-Community Camera Adventure such as videos, posters, mobiles, maps, models, collages, calendars, date books, scrapbooks, or whatever educators prefer to create. Nevertheless, significant debriefing should occur after this activity occurs, for being placed in a situation as "the other" could have sensitive ramifications and/or could also reinforce the actual stereotypes that the activity

(Continued)

(Continued)

hopes to debunk. We usually share and discuss what was learned from this activity using a whole group discussion format, but there are other ways to do this as well.

Teachers' Responses to the Home-Community Camera Adventure

Teachers who completed the Home-Community Camera Adventure often expressed emotions such as anxiety, excitement, curiosity, fear, apprehension, nervousness, and uncertainty at the outset. One preservice teacher wondered why since "I only see these students once a week. Why do I need to learn all this about them? " Others did not want to be intrusive. In fact, one mentioned, "I didn't want anyone who saw me to think I was up to something while taking pictures." Still other teachers voiced worry and concern about being able to find a community about which they could report, although being fearful was not an inhibiting factor for them. One said, "I was worried that I was not going to be able to find a community with good information. I was not apprehensive about going into the community because I understood the reality of it."

When asked if the communities lived up to their prior expectations, several participants expressed being "pleasantly surprised." One stated,

> The community was nothing like I expected. I thought that I would see a lot of smoking and hear a lot of loud talking and cursing. The community was not like that at all! It was calm. . . . We just saw people going about their own business.

Another noted, "Within the first five minutes of the project, my begrudging attitude turned into interest."

Another teacher who completed the Camera Adventure near a historically Black college mentioned that he "didn't expect there to be such a strong community aspect. I guess I just didn't know or hadn't thought about it, but [what I saw] was very encouraging." However, other teachers were not surprised at what they found. In fact, one said,

> For the most part, the community is what I expected it to be. The houses were small as well as the yards, and some lots are very run down. Also there are some vacant run-down houses that are not safe for anybody to live in. I have been through neighborhoods like this in my hometown, so it was not very different or eye-opening for me.

What shocks teachers most about their findings from the Home-Community Camera Adventure is quite revealing. "Gang graffiti shocked me the most, and the fact that it looked like it had been there for a long time" was one response.

Another teacher who asked parental permission for her student to accompany her in the community was shocked at the kindness of the parents. She said, "The thing that shocked me the most was the fact that the parents welcomed me into their home. They were very friendly, and allowed the student to take me around the neighborhood." The fact that she was not perceived to be intrusive was also surprising to her. Material possessions in low-income neighborhoods made impressions as well. One participant revealed, the "BMW with rims sitting in front of this run-down apartment complex seemed very out of place." Significant impact was made on one preservice teacher depending on which side of the road he happened to be standing. "What shocked me the most was how there could be run-down houses that looked almost uninhabitable on one side of the road and then brand new two-story houses on the other side of the road."

What participants learned from the Home-Community Camera Adventure varied. Several were determined not to be as judgmental about students and their families as they were before and "not make assumptions about students and their backgrounds until I know better." A preservice teacher noted how the Home-Community Camera Adventure made a lasting impression on her about perseverance. She said,

> I think that this assignment will stick with me throughout my student teaching and career as a teacher. I had never been in a community such as this, and after visiting this place, I have to say that it made me think. Getting through school is hard for some people, but getting an education and living in a place that requires constant police patrol and is dangerous at times is a whole other feat in itself. And some kids keep coming to school and wanting to learn.

Another teacher recognized the effect that stereotypical attitudes about others could have on her and wanted to dismiss them before they became a part of her professional dispositions. She went on to say,

> This experience will force me to get to know every child. When I get my roster in the summer, I will make it an effort to ask questions, drive around neighborhoods, etc. If I can dispel stereotypes before they even step foot in my room, I feel I have already started to make a difference.

Challenges to Consider

An obvious challenge in asking educators to complete the Home-Community Camera Adventure includes both silent and vocal resistance. This reaction is driven by fear of the unknown. Usually, educators have only heard about the communities of their students, especially about students who live in low-income areas. Media descriptions of such neighborhoods, particularly those that are reported where

(Continued)

(Continued)

crime or violent activity has taken place, cause educators to be concerned about their safety. An additional fear that needs considered is the feeling of being the ethnic *minority* in a location. For many educators, they have always moved in spaces where they were in the ethnic *majority*, which provided them with safety in numbers, confidence in knowledge of their collective worldviews and their where-abouts, and complete understanding of the language used and the cultural nuances practiced in their world. Moving outside of their comfort zone creates, for some, a high level of discomfort because they do not know what to expect. Nonetheless, the value of the Home-Community Camera Adventure is that educators make a genuine effort to view their students' communities through strengths-based eyes. They have an opportunity to speak with community members with whom they would otherwise not have the chance to engage with and learn from. Finally, educators have the opportunity to reconsider some of the previously held beliefs they had about a community and its inhabitants and, instead, make a clear statement of support for their students who live in the communities visited.

Another challenge is that the community itself may reject the presence of "strangers." Obviously, strangers, especially those of a different ethnic group, will be the object of intense stares. Some people will question the purpose of educators' presence, and they may suspect ulterior motives. In addition, in our experience there were times when managers of public-housing communities would not allow teachers to walk through the community, even when we explained the activity and provided written instructions for it. No doubt one of the reasons is because "the other" is seen usually by members of the community as law enforcement and/or emergency services, which means that trouble is brewing. Some managers appeared poised to challenge teachers' motives for doing the activity for fear of positioning the community in a negative light. To help alleviate this challenge, we suggest notifying the community managers first to let them know what you are planning. Educators can also alert their students of desire to do this project, and with their parents/guardians' permission, ask that they go with you on the Camera Adventure. If resistance continues, choose another community.

Note: The Home-Community Camera Adventure was developed and used with permission from a leadership organization and adapted accordingly.

ACTIVITY 7.2 WALKING A MILE IN ANOTHER'S SHOES

The community adventure activity we call Walking a Mile in Another's Shoes is another cultural immersion experience that is beneficial for both beginning and experienced educators (Cooper, 2007). This type of cultural immersion experience is designed to provide educators with experience dealing with real-life scenarios that involve things their students and their families might also experience.

Objectives

- To generate empathy, but certainly not sympathy, for the lived experiences of students and their families
- To think about and learn from their assigned scenario so they can use what they learned to help motivate their students and encourage them to achieve in school.
- To reframe what appears to be adversity in families' lives and think about how coping strategies in such situations can also be viewed as ways of demonstrating strength-based learning

Planning and Preparation

Each Walking a Mile in Another's Shoes scenario was developed and used with permission from a leadership organization and adapted accordingly. It is especially important to note that agency officials were contacted prior to any teacher's visit so that actual services and resources would not be formally allocated to them. Each written scenario was tailored for the relevant community setting, and in some cases, it was designed in cooperation with personnel from the particular agencies involved. For example, the program manager of Food and Nutrition Services at the county Department of Social Services helped to design the activity related to the acquisition of food stamps. Also, given the state of the economy in recent years, telephone calls were made by the teachers to set up appointments rather than having them just appear unannounced at an agency office. Although their treatment did not differ from actual clients or persons in need of aid, this appointment procedure made it easier for agency personnel to meet with the growing number of persons in true need of services. See Resources 7.1, 7.2, and 7.3 on the companion website for this book for examples of three possible scenarios you can adapt as needed for your setting. Each written scenario also includes a set of reflective questions.

Based on our experience, we decided that educators who completed this activity could not always choose which adventure to complete because they might choose one that did not take them out of their comfort zone. However, once teachers heard the choices of adventures, they had the opportunity to share their reasons for discomfort in doing them or to reveal prior experiences with them. For instance, some teachers had used public transportation as their primary source of mobility. Others already had personal experience with going to the Department of Social Services and seeking aid at some point in their life. In these cases, scenarios that involved such activities were not appropriate for those particular people, so they chose another scenario.

Instructions for Participants

When we use these community-based learning experiences each educator is given a scenario that includes experiences such as those described in Resources 7.1,

(Continued)

(Continued)

7.2, and 7.3, and three to four weeks is allocated for educators to complete their designated activity. As with the Camera Adventure, Walking a Mile in Another's Shoes was equally successful when educators went with a partner or individually. The list of potential community adventures usually includes the following:

- Using public transportation to apply for an hourly wage job
- Applying for subsidized child care (as either a two-parent or single-parent head of household families)
- Applying for subsidized housing
- Eating at a shelter for the homeless
- Applying for food stamps
- Taking a police ride
- Enrolling a child in school as a gay couple
- Being low income and seeking health care
- Attending an Alcoholics Anonymous meeting and/or a Narcotics Anonymous meeting
- Seeking services as an immigrant or refugee
- Seeking resources while living in public housing
- Seeking a job/observing at a job fair

Teachers' Reponses to Walking a Mile in Another's Shoes

Since some participants could not select their community adventure, some felt "apprehensive," "anxious," and "nervous." For example, a preservice teacher who took the police ride felt "incredibly apprehensive of the police." However, there was a reason for her to feel this way. She explained, "Over the course of a year, I was pulled over three times and harassed for nonspecified reasons. One evening, I was followed (but not pulled over) while returning to my parents' house—perhaps I posed a threat because I looked 'out of place.' I experience a lot of stress whenever the police are near me." Another teacher who took the police ride was "definitely a bit anxious because I was not sure what to expect." Once she got in the police car, she did "feel an initial wave of fear." Entering the waiting room at the Department of Social Services caused one teacher to feel "like such a poser . . . very uncomfortable taking time from the people there." At the Narcotics Anonymous meeting, another, who had been a former rock band member, anticipated what her experience would be like:

> Before attending a Narcotics Anonymous meeting, I envisioned hearing stories about struggle and despair from a varied group of people. I expected to be nervous myself because I would be in the group but not an addict; I was afraid that it would be obvious. . . . Many of my anticipations held true on my arrival and participation.

Though later, she found that

A loving and accepting tone was the standard way of communication—a common understanding among all of the participants. Everyone functioned as an equal, no matter their education or background. The greeting is always a hug and a kind word. There also seemed to be an unspoken but mutual understanding about the common experience and sentiments about the nature of narcotic addiction: fear of relapse and the remaining hope that they will fully recover. It came as a very powerful understanding to me—I could not recall any other setting I had been in where such a variety of people shared such a strong, loving connection with one another (outside of rock 'n roll concerts).

Though nervousness prevailed in those completing the Walking a Mile in Another's Shoes scenarios, some media-driven stereotypical descriptions were unveiled. At a different Narcotics Anonymous meeting, one participant expressed great surprise.

I imagined a room full of bikers with long hair, beards, and tattoos. I imagined a rough looking bunch in their mid to late 40s much like drug users are sometimes portrayed on television and in movies. For some reason, I did not envision any women or young people, nor any white-collar types. I imagined depressed looking people with sad stories who have lived rough lives. I expected to feel awkward and planned to sneak in and sit in the back of the room. I expected coffee drinking and cigarette smoking. When I actually made it into the meeting, I saw very little of what I had anticipated.

Frustration ensued for several teachers while they were immersed in their assigned activities. Riding the bus became an exercise in aggravation for one. While it took her twice as long as normal to take the bus, her bus arrived early on that particular day, causing her to wait an additional 10 minutes before the next bus arrived. Since she was not feeling well on another day, she missed the connection and had to wait another half an hour. Additionally, being confined to purchasing food with food stamps also became annoying and disappointing. Further, when teachers actually visited a locally infamous public-housing neighborhood, they initially felt that they were "imposing on people's lives." Nonetheless, when they discovered that they had to access human resources in the neighborhood to find the answers to their questions, they found out that the community's inhabitants were more than happy to help them. In fact, the people in the neighborhood were glad that the teachers considered them to be experts of their lives and valued their opinions. Moreover, several participants realized they had to overcome their

(Continued)

(Continued)

personal barriers to discover the information they needed. One summarized her feelings by saying,

> I believe the biggest barrier we faced was our own personal struggle to feel OK with walking up to people. I think once we had talked with one group that barrier was broken down, and we felt a little more at ease with confronting others in the neighborhood.

When determining what was gained from this cultural immersion experience and how it could be used in future educational experiences, some teachers tended to want to help make students' living conditions better. "Having extra snacks in the room," "keeping a safe and structured environment," and "being sensitive to every family's situation" were all good strategies to help ease the strain of some families' socioeconomic, psychological, and emotional plights. Nevertheless, others realized different benefits from being culturally immersed in their activities, not only for themselves but also for the students with whom they interact with daily. In fact, one preservice teacher recounted, "This assignment really helped me to put things into perspective. It made me examine my own reality relative to the reality of others." Another said,

> The experience has reminded me of the realities of life. That so many people have real troubles at home and that so many of these homes have children living in them. I know that, as a teacher, there is nothing I can do to change the conditions in which they live. I won't make excuses for them but I will be compassionate and try to help them achieve in school despite the hardships placed on them in their lives.

Still another teacher remembered the importance of families and the impressions they were left with, especially when differences in race/ethnicity are involved.

> I was reminded that it's important to start off on the right foot with the families of our future students. As the manager [of the public housing units] said, it's hard to climb out of the hole of a bad first impression, especially as a White teacher with students of color. Being flexible with parental involvement is key, too.

Transformative Effects of Community Adventures

Reflecting on the impact of these activities, teachers revealed transformations in themselves because of their experiences with the communities of their students. One teacher pointed to these activities to help her reflect on the cultural relevance of curriculum materials she used and how she could change the textbook's content to more readily help her students identify with it. While reading a picture book to her students, she recognized that what the book considered a house was not the same one for many of her students. She went on to explain, "Not all my kids lived in houses. I don't think hardly any of them did. They lived in apartments. They lived in trailers and other places." Therefore, she decided,

> If I hadn't known more about my kids' neighborhoods and wanted to know more because of the community activities we did that I probably would have brushed that off, and I would have said now draw a picture of your house or something like that. But we discussed different places people could live. We drew. I had them do a journal, and they drew where they lived, and I remember one of my students drew a picture of his trailer, and it had wheels on it, and it said, "I live in a trailer. I love my trailer."

Another teacher noted the confidence she gained in going into the home communities of her learners:

> Throughout this year, I worked with a lot of children who weren't used to a teacher going to their house or going to their soccer games or their basketball games and really putting themselves out there or even calling home a lot. They just really didn't see. Every time I came to a game, they were shocked, like they thought I wasn't going to come. It put me in situations where I normally would be uncomfortable, but I went anyway just because I knew that it was important. I think that really helped with the students because one particular child had been retained, and she was so upset throughout the whole year, but I continuously went to her basketball games and called her grandma and called her mom, and she ended up doing great. I mean she comes to my door now and says hello to me every morning, too. I think that going into her community to see about her really made a difference. She wasn't used to a teacher making that kind of step, that next step in putting yourself out there and tearing your walls down with people.

Another teacher remembered how the activities helped her recognize that parents play a vital role in educating their children. The activities also aided her in building stronger relationships with the parents of her students. She recalled that when attempting to contact a parent,

> I found that if I brought her [the mother] into the process of her child's education that she would be more positive. This was a parent who was never involved with the school. She never came to conferences. She wouldn't return phone calls to the school or anything at the previous school she had been in. At this school, I guess I was just a pest, and I kept calling and kept asking. But the very first thing I'd always say to her was what do you think you can do to help me or what would you feel would help your son. I felt like she had a role in it, and I felt that she was important. I think that just came from the experiences that I had doing Walking a Mile, the Camera Adventure, and the Privilege Walk and looking at what people bring to education and what the role of parents needs to be.

Still another teacher learned about the importance of knowing herself while doing the activities. She said,

> Knowing myself and knowing the people in this community [her school community] have made a difference, and really those experiences [Privilege Walk, Camera Adventure, and Walking a Mile] have taught me how to go about getting to know the community, how to jump in, not just sit along the sides and teach and teach everyone the same way but actually dive in and make yourself a part of their family. I still have several students who I'm keeping in contact with over the summer with their families. Some of them are still calling me and coming to see me even now that they are in middle school.

Challenges in Completing Walking a Mile in Another's Shoes

As stated earlier, authenticity is required to gain the most benefit from this community-based activity. Collaboration with agency officials where needed is not really an issue. We have found that these professionals have been more than willing to assist us with such activities, especially if they are approached without a deficit view. In fact, many agency officials have been pleased that we offer this kind of activity for educators. However, making sure that others within the agency follow through with the authentic engagement has, at times, been a challenge. To be more specific, educators must schedule an appointment to be seen by appropriate agency personnel, who are told not to enter the client/educator into the "system," but to consider the educator just as they would a real applicant. Sometimes there is a breakdown in communication because the personnel, at times, have not carried out the activity as it was originally planned. Then engagement becomes more of an information session where the educator asks the questions and the agency employee serves as the interviewee. Although this is not a bad idea, the educators have not planned questions to ask. Furthermore, the goal of the activity—to walk a mile in another's shoes to experience what it is like for the parents/guardians of their students—may not be achieved.

Fear is also an emotion that has accompanied this activity. Some educators expressed fear of being seen while applying for social services or just being seen in the facility by others. General discomfort related to sitting in a waiting area for long periods was also another challenge for some, and lying or using imagined scenarios for the activity left a few educators uncomfortable.

Perhaps the biggest challenge for educators was scheduling the activity. Teachers and administrators' lives are busy. Given that many activities require completion during the workweek, a workday or an early release day for professional development can be used to complete the activities. By providing this time for teachers and other school personnel to do this activity, administrators recognize the importance and need for this kind of professional development to occur.

SUMMARY OF KEY POINTS

In this chapter, we described the changing composition of families and how our views of families can influence how we engage with our learners. We also emphasize the importance of partnering with parents, guardians, and community members, as they are our learners' first teachers. We introduced community-based learning as a pedagogical tool for educators to further enhance their interactions with parents and families and to strengthen instructional methods through the infusion of knowledge of students' home communities. By doing so, educators become more critically culturally competent in meeting the needs of their learners. Two specific community-based cultural immersion activities were shared with the reactions of teachers to their experiences with them:

- Activity 7.1 Home-Community Camera Adventure
- Activity 7.2 Walking a Mile in Another's Shoes

REFLECTION AND EXTENSION

- In preparation for having educators complete the activities described in this chapter, pick one of the previous activities, either the Home-Community Camera Adventure or Walking a Mile in Another's Shoes, to complete yourself. Reflect on the experience and on how you might add to or modify the activity for your situation.
- Make arrangements and prepare a scenario for a different community adventure similar to the examples described previously for the activity called Walking a Mile in Another's Shoes. Choose something relevant to your community.

ONLINE EXTENSIONS

The Home-Community Camera Adventure can also be completed, shared, and even debriefed when doing online professional development. Using the same instructions, educators can work with a partner or in a small group (we recommend no more than three per group) to visit the home communities of their learners with their digital cameras in tow. Again, educators should be prepared with written directions, just in case questions arise about their presence in communities. After all pictures have been taken, educators can use programs like PowerPoint, Publisher, or PhotoStory or free, online resources such as VoiceThread to prepare either individual or group presentations about what they learned about the communities they visited. Their electronic presentations can then be shared using whatever course management system the school district supports, on a blog for the diversity workshop, or saved for sharing when the group meets face-to-face. Alternative formats for sharing results of the Home-Community Camera Adventure, such as posters, mobiles, maps, models, calendars, date books, videos, scrapbooks, or whatever educators prefer to create, can also be shared online via videos that they create and upload to the course management system or even to TeacherTube. They can also share their videos using Animoto or other increasingly available tools available free on the Internet.

FOCUS FOR PROFESSIONAL LEARNING COMMUNITIES (PLCs)

PLCs are ideal groups to engage in community-based learning experiences. Choosing scenarios that match some of situations that their students and families experience daily will certainly help the members of the PLC become better able to understand and meet their students' learning needs at school. Once again, however, we must remind leaders and members of the PLC to look at their community-based adventure from a strength-based versus deficit-based perspective and to determine actions they can take based on what they learn, rather than to just feel sympathy. PLCs can contact the school's social worker and/or home–school coordinator for assistance in setting up some scenarios if no one in the PLC feels qualified to do so. These staff members can also help the PLC with debriefing what was learned from their community-based adventure.

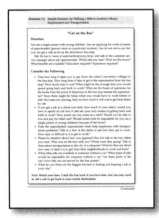

8

Bringing It All Together

How Do We Maximize Teaching
and Learning Opportunities?

Introduction

This final chapter includes a sample lesson, a suggested plan for professional development for building critical cultural competence in professional learning communities (PLCs), and a longer-term plan to show how various activities from this book can be used toward leading transformation of school cultures so that they are more culturally responsive for diverse learners. Measures and indicators for success are also shared for ongoing evaluation of the effectiveness of professional development efforts. We also discuss how culturally responsive teaching (Gay, 2002; Nieto & Bode, 2008; Villegas & Lucas, 2002) relates to critical cultural competence. In the process, we emphasize the importance of leaders of professional development engaging in critical reflection so they can effectively guide the development of other educators toward critical cultural competence. And we reiterate how professional development can and should be a catalyst for transformative practices, the need for administrative support, and information about how the change process works when innovative ideas, such as those presented in this book, are introduced.

Connecting Culturally Responsive Pedagogy and Critical Cultural Competence

One way critical cultural competence can be demonstrated is through the ongoing, committed practice of culturally responsive teaching (Milner, 2010). This pedagogy considers students' cultures in the delivering the curriculum in ways that are nonjudgmental and inclusive of the backgrounds of students for providing more relevant instruction in the classroom. By acknowledging the importance of students' cultures, educators respect the home-community cultures that students bring with them to school. Further, with sensitivity to the complexity of cultural identities, educators can more ably integrate students' cultural experiences, values, and understandings into the teaching and learning environment (Brown-Jeffy & Cooper, 2011).

In fact, the following descriptions of culturally responsive educators overlap 100% with characteristics and actions of educators who have developed critical cultural competence. Therefore, as you work to bring cultural responsive practices into classrooms and schools, you are also working to develop critical cultural competence. The two go hand in hand.

Culturally responsive educators are not color-blind. In fact, they reject the color-blind construct. They recognize their cultural backgrounds and how their backgrounds might enrich and—at the same time—limit understanding their students. They recognize the ethnic groups their students come from, and purposefully incorporate students' languages and cultures in their teaching. Culturally responsive educators, who are educators with critical cultural competence, acknowledge that being color-blind is detrimental to their students' academic, social, emotional, and psychological development and that it also limits their professional development and dispositions. By rejecting the color-blind construct, educators see students for who they are and who they could become, and educators value the strengths they acquire from their diverse cultural backgrounds.

Culturally responsive educators attempt to negotiate the cultural conflict that their positions of power often represent. It is easy to remain comfortable in one's culture; however, it is more difficult to consider others' backgrounds. Culturally competent educators who strive to be culturally responsive accept that not all their students are of the ethnic majority, are members of the middle class, are fluent English-language speakers, and are above-average learners. They incorporate various examples and scenarios of what life is like for the diverse members of their classrooms in sensitive and respectful ways in their teaching and other interactions with students, and they make the "language of power" (Delpit, 1995) explicit for all students so they know ways to be successful in schools and other institutions.

Culturally responsive educators reject the myth of meritocracy. Arguably, most educators believe in hard work, but they realize that because of institutional and structural barriers that have been sustained historically, not everyone who works hard gets what they want and is able to succeed. For many, the myth of meritocracy is just that—a myth. Culturally responsive educators encourage students to work hard, they provide the content and skills their students need, and they coach their students to believe in themselves even when it appears, at times, that others do not. Culturally responsive educators advocate for their students, and they work hard to empower students and families to challenge institutional structures that are not equitable. In essence, culturally responsive educators help their students "keep on keepin' on" despite barriers that seem insurmountable.

Culturally responsive educators reject deficit-based thinking. They refuse to allow deficit beliefs about students to cloud their thinking or influence their professional practice. They continue to hold high expectations of all students. They value the identities of their students and treat them equitably. They also believe that their students can achieve. They educate the whole child in developmentally appropriate ways, and they maintain strong, positive relationships with students and their families (Brown-Jeffy & Cooper, 2011), as do educators who have critical cultural competence. Culturally responsive educators are not afraid to take risks for what they believe and do, and they understand that while many culturally responsive practices are considered "just good teaching" (Ladson-Billings, 1995), culturally responsive educators go above and beyond traditional practices to include and involve the families and communities of their students.

Taking Risks to Develop Critical Cultural Competence

The activities included in this book range from those that are safe to those that involve risks. We believe the readings and videos suggested in this book provide safe ways to help educators become more culturally competent and culturally responsive in their professional practice, but they are not enough because they do not provide actual experiences with students, families, and communities, and they can be mis-educative if not discussed critically. Reading case studies, participating in book clubs, and engaging in role plays are usually safe activities, and we believe they are valuable learning experiences because they offer opportunities to problem solve situations that could occur in classrooms and schools. While listening to guest speakers may engender feelings of empathy, it takes more hands-on and immersive experiences to develop true empathy by asking, "What if I were in their shoes? What would I do if I were in this situation?" To begin to develop critical cultural competence individual reflections and group processing are needed to make the most of the activities suggested in this book, but they must be guided by a knowledgeable and critically culturally competent leader/facilitator.

Understanding "who you are in this thing called diversity" is also necessary in examining one's individual dispositions about and experiences with diversity. Cultural autobiographies require factual statements about who you are, including diversities over which you have no control, as does participating in the Privilege Walk. Revealing your beliefs, philosophy, or vision as an educator helps define what you believe about teaching to and learning for today's diverse students and how you hope to enact what you believe in your class or school. Such activities require deeper levels of reflection and revealing one's beliefs and values. What is learned about the self using some of the activities in Chapters 2 and 3 depends on how much you want to reveal about yourself, and we believe these activities are necessary to develop critical cultural competence because such investigations can uncover personal biases and prejudices about students and their families that may otherwise remain hidden. Therefore, committing to learning more about oneself from engaging wholeheartedly in these activities is, to a degree, a risk-taking venture, as is undertaking action research for changing your practices—especially when the goal is to make them more culturally responsive.

After interrogating yourself, finding out about your students is the next step in developing critical cultural competence and being a culturally responsive educator. Web-based investigations and fact sheets are safe ways to gain knowledge about students' national origins, religions, and exceptionalities, but this information is a useful first step in helping educators make informed connections with students and their families. However, what can be learned directly from students' and their families' by completing the ABCs Project is much more powerful because students' individual lived experiences are very likely to be different from what is stated on a fact sheet based on research about a group. By wholeheartedly engaging in the activities in Chapters 4 and 5, your cultural knowledge base is expanded, intentional linkages are made to narrow the cultural divide between you and your students; therefore, doing them can lead to making you a more critically culturally competent educator.

However, the journey to developing critical cultural competence must involve some additional risk taking, which requires educators to leave the comfort of the school and enter the home communities of their students. After all, students' homes and communities are the environments where their initial learning takes place and the locations that frame and give meaning to how students learn, interpret, and navigate the world around them. We maintain that the best educators "know" what their students experience and how they feel. Furthermore, considering parents, families, and communities as copartners in educating children is crucial for acknowledging, understanding, and accepting diverse ways of seeing, knowing, and doing. Home and community visits invite educators to leave their comfort zones to see how their students live. Just being able to discuss with students what you see in the neighborhoods in which they live encourages connections with them and their families. However, neighborhood bus tours and doing the Home-Community Camera Adventure are only meaningful if educators interact with community members. Completing experiences in Chapters 6 and 7, especially like those in the Walking a Mile in Another's Shoes activity, can give teachers and administrators additional insights about how students and families navigate and negotiate their lives outside of school, therefore, a lens to better understand how resilience can be demonstrated inside school. Also, the risks of visiting your students' communities and having experiences their families have in surviving outside the educational arena could engender discussions never before raised about why situations like prejudice, inequality, and institutional racism persist. Discussion about such experiences could lead to seeking solutions to institutional and structural injustices never considered before these community adventures occurred. Undertaking some risk can only help educators become more skilled in culturally responsive teaching and in developing more critical cultural competence, so we believe that teachers and administrators need to leave their school to go into the community of their learners. This may feel daring for some, but it is absolutely required to become a more culturally responsive and critically culturally competent educator.

Inspiring Critical Reflection and Awareness

One key feature of the activities discussed in this book is the emphasis on critical reflection. Facilitators' feedback is essential in ensuring a nonthreatening environment where everyone feels comfortable examining their assumptions, biases, and beliefs without feeling judged. It is the facilitator's role to generate a sense of "positive restlessness" (Kuh, 2007), through which educators are recognized for their efforts toward reflection and yet challenged to develop their critical cultural awareness. Facilitators need to be aware of several considerations to achieve the balance of being *positive* and generating *restlessness*.

First, building trust is foundational in establishing an environment that allows for constructive feedback. Trust entails at least two dimensions: the process and the intention. Both facilitators and participants need to trust that they are engaged in the process of reflection, rather than seeking the right answers for the reflection questions. Educators' genuine intention of sharing what they truly believe is important to protect, even though some may express values we do not necessarily agree with as facilitators (such as the teacher statements highlighted by Milner, 2010, discussed in Chapter 1).

To build trust among facilitators and participants, at the beginning of the professional development, facilitators can engage educators in sharing their criteria for quality discussions. Sharing personal stories and experiences by both the facilitator and the participants are also great ways to build trust from the very beginning because participants become more comfortable sharing their individual stories and the facilitator presents a model for such sharing. To successfully lead all the activities mentioned in this book, therefore, we would strongly encourage leaders of professional development go through all of them first and record their thoughts for the suggested debriefing questions.

Second, to provide scaffolding through feedback, facilitators need to be aware of the levels of reflection and how they are developed. Constructive feedback challenges participants within their zone of proximal development (Vygotsky, 1978). When applied to guiding reflection, facilitators need to be aware of levels of reflection to guide and facilitate development beyond knowledge toward critical cultural competence.

Many educators have studied the development of reflection as an important process in learning. Schön (1983), for example, proposed two frames of reflection: reflection-in-action and reflection-on-action. In teaching, *reflection-in-action* requires educators to have a habit of reflection and be able to reflect before they react to professional issues on the spot. *Reflection-on-action*, on the other hand, could occur before or after an action in teaching. Building on Schön's distinction of reflection-in-action versus reflection-on-action, Hatton and Smith (1995) proposed a framework that identified levels of reflection. Knowing about levels of reflection is very helpful as we observe and facilitate the development of reflection from technical to critical and contextualized in discussions about equity and diversity. In Resource 8.1, we provided *Hatton and*

Smith's framework and some sample scaffolding questions that facilitators could use to encourage educators to deepen reflection during discussion.

Third, facilitators need to be skillful in using verbal and nonverbal communication strategies to maximize interactions among educators. The active listening strategies introduced in Chapter 5 are skills that facilitators should practice when leading debriefing activities. Because typical interactions between facilitators and participants are not one-on-one dialogues, it is important for facilitators to engage educators in discussions rather than following the traditional question-response-feedback pattern.

Figure 8.1 Reflection Levels (adapted from Hatton & Smith, 1995; Schön, 1983; Shulman, 1987)

Types of Reflection		Characteristics	Scaffolding Questions
Reflection-on-action	Technical reflection	• Focusing on personal and task concerns • Examining the use of essential skills or generic competencies	• Why did that happen? • What led to your judgment in this case? • How would others view this issue?
	Descriptive reflection	• Providing reasons/justification for events or actions • Drawing from literature or personal experiences • Recognizing alternate viewpoints	• What could be another interpretation of what happened? • How would you describe some different viewpoints on this issue?
	Dialogic reflection	• Stepping back from the events or actions • Weighing competing claims and viewpoints • Exploring alternative explanations or solutions	• How does the larger sociopolitical context impact our understanding, perception, or feelings in this case?
	Critical reflection	• Demonstrating an awareness of the connectedness of events and actions with larger historic and sociopolitical contexts	• What if _____? How would you respond to that?
Reflection-in-action	Contextualized reflection	• Dealing with on-the-spot professional issues (may recall the events or actions and share them) • Drawing from any of the previous types of reflection	

When educators are self-selecting their turn in conversation, sufficient wait time is especially important. Wait time can be intentionally built into the debriefing so that all educators are prepared to share their thoughts. This is especially important when discussing controversial issues or those that could cause discomfort for some educators. Simple think-pair-share activities can be used in this case to allow time for processing. When providing time for educators to think about the questions, it is always a good idea to not only verbally state the questions but also have them on either handouts or projected on an overhead so participants can see them as they listen to others' responses as well.

Another effective strategy to facilitate critical conversations is the use of the Paideia seminar format (www.paideia.org/), which guides formal dialogue by asking open-ended questions planned by the facilitator. Although such Socratic seminars are typically used in K–12 settings to facilitate critical thinking about a specific text related to a content topic, the Paideia format can be adapted and used to facilitate discussions for critical cultural competence development where educators can be encouraged to share multiple perspectives regarding a common text, object, or experience.

Fourth, careful planning needs to be accompanied with thoughtfully adaptive instruction so the discussion can be truly participant centered. The concept of thoughtful adaptation was first discussed in studies of effectiveness of reading teachers (Duffy & Hoffman, 1999). Thoughtfully adaptive teachers were observed to make spontaneous decisions based on the ongoing feedback they received from students' responses. It is not just on-the-spot decision making without planning. On the contrary, the teacher overprepares with various materials and methods and is able to apply one that maximizes student learning based on ongoing assessment during interactions and observations.

Applying the concept of thoughtful adaptation to discussion facilitation, facilitators also need to be fully aware of various possible directions discussions may lead and be prepared with questions that could challenge all educators and promote critical thinking. Experiences leading and facilitating discussions definitely are necessary in developing the habit of thoughtful adaptation. However, experience itself is not sufficient. Facilitators need to be mindful in their observations of educators and engage in ongoing reflection-in-action themselves to be more conscientious about developing their skills in leading educators to critical reflections.

Finally, facilitators need to be explicit in promoting the process of the discussion to the metacognitive level for educators to transfer the group discussion process into a habit of critical self-reflection. The way facilitators guide discussions should also model processes that educators could engage themselves in self-monitoring and self-questioning to develop critical reflection as a habit of mind. The ultimate purpose of providing professional development on critical cultural competence for is not for educators to stop at experiencing and sharing their thoughts regarding the specific professional development activities. True critical cultural competence is their ability to be critically aware and be willing and able to serve as change agents in their daily interactions with their peers, administrators, students, families, and community partners. Therefore, transfer from facilitators' debriefing to educators' self-monitoring and questioning of beliefs, assumptions, language use, and behaviors needs to be made explicit before, during, or after every discussion. In addition to learning through well-planned and guided discussions, facilitators also need to bring educators' awareness of their reflective process to the metacognitive level to allow for this transfer. This is done by analyzing the discussion and making the participants consciously aware of where they started and where they still need to go to develop critical cultural competence.

Transforming Professional Practice

Of course, besides developing a habit of critical reflection, it must be clear to all those involved that the transformation required to develop critical cultural competence calls for collaboration, support, and strategic planning. Those leading professional development, including building-level administrators and district-level administrators, and the participants in professional development sessions and in PLCs have to work collaboratively toward the same goals (Hord, 1997). No doubt, the support and leadership of the school principal is important in how faculty and staff react to diversity in a school. This means that the goal of becoming critically culturally competent has to be explicit and understood by all involved, and all the leaders at the school (and hopefully the district) have to be on board and engaged in the process. Further, those who lead professional development, as well as other teacher leaders and administrators, have to model critical cultural competence throughout the process. They have to be change agents themselves or, at the very least, be more than willing to support change, but also they have to understand that change does not happen quickly through one-time or one-size-fits-all forms of professional development.

School leaders have to know and be supportive of long-term professional development, maybe even extending over a year or two, to see real change from awareness of diversity and the need for cultural competence to see critical cultural competence in action. Also, they have to be supportive of ongoing conversations about critical cultural competence and of many professional learning opportunities that are followed by serious reflection and practice with feedback. Furthermore, they have to understand that not everyone begins the journey of becoming a critically culturally competent educator in the same place or develops at the same rate. Therefore, professional development leaders, teacher leaders, and administrators engaged in this process have to seriously consider the value of allowing, and even encouraging, different groups to start with and engage in different activities suggested in this book at different times. In other words, they have to seriously consider differentiating professional development experiences based on what individuals, PLCs, or other groups of educators are ready for.

Using Rogers's Adoption of Innovation Theory

Everett M. Rogers's (2003) adoption of innovation theory, which explains the ways individuals and organizations react to innovations, is very useful when planning professional development, especially the kind of professional development that is designed to be transformative such as developing critical cultural competence. Rogers's work indicates that change takes the form of a bell-shaped curve, suggesting that not all those involved in the change are going to adapt to or adopt change at the same rate, a point we made earlier. Rogers also indicates that each person's willingness and ability to adopt an innovation depends on his or her interest, the value placed on the innovation, and previous experience or interaction with that innovation. Therefore, those working to help others develop critical cultural competence need to consider and account for the following five types of individual change (Rogers, 2003), which are shown in Figure 8.2 with the percentage of individuals who typically fall into each category during the implementation of an innovation.

Rogers's (2003) theory about adoption of innovations and new ideas tells us that each person's willingness and ability to change varies, so participants' interest, value placed on the innovation, and prior experiences with that innovation need considered when deciding on activities to start the change process toward critical cultural competence. For example, surfacing educators' prior beliefs and experiences with diversity issues needs to happen through the activities, reflections, and discussions like those discussed in Chapters 2 through 5, but some may need to begin by reading and discussing books and/or videos to develop awareness. Those educators who are ready and willing to go out into the community should be encouraged to do so.

Figure 8.2 Percentages of Types of Adopters of Change (adapted from Rogers, 2003)

Innovators are brave people leading the change (2.5%).

Early adopters are respected people and opinion leaders willing to try innovations in careful ways (13.5%).

Early majority are thoughtful but careful in accepting change, but they do accept change more quickly than the average person (34%).

Late majority are people who are skeptical and only use new ideas once the majority are using them (34%).

Laggards are more traditional and are often critical of new ideas (16%).

However, although they may only be ready for the activities in Chapter 6, they can be encouraged to go beyond the safety of their classrooms and schools to complete the Home-Community Camera Adventure and/or the Walking a Mile in Another's Shoes activity described in Chapter 7. The innovators and early adopters, to use Rogers's terms, can then share what they have learned with others and motivate the early and late majority to move forward.

Rogers (2003) also says that a critical mass of adopters is needed to convince the mainstream of the importance of the innovation and that empowering educators and giving them decision-making opportunities improves their professional commitment and affects positive evaluation of change initiatives (Hall & Hord, 1987). Given this information, it is important to support individuals moving forward when they are ready and not punish or threaten those who are slow with or resistant to adopting innovative and new ideas. Therefore, we recommend differentiating the activities offered to educators by giving them options and, perhaps, adding some of the activities from this book to their annual professional learning goals as one strategy. We also recommend assessing the needs of various grade-level teams, departments, and/or PLCs to see where they are with their knowledge of and experience with diversity issues before suggesting activities to help them build critical cultural competence. Specific suggestions about how and when to do this are described later in this chapter.

Using the Concerns-Based Adoption Model (CBAM)

The concerns-based adoption model (CBAM), which was developed and researched in professional development settings (Hall & Hord, 1987; Hord, Rutherford, Huling-Austin, & Hall, 1987), is another useful model for deciding where to begin when group members have different prior experiences with diversity. CBAM is a process-oriented approach that examines individual reactions to change, especially in educational contexts. For more than 20 years, CBAM has provided information and guidance to professional developers and other school leaders as they begin to think about introducing changes. We believe this model is also useful in planning and differentiating professional development opportunities. In particular, CBAM helps explain the way the process of change works for individuals because it offers insights about where people are in the change process by paying attention to the types of questions they ask and the concerns they articulate. For example, early questions may be about what critical cultural competence is all about, and answers should include clear definitions and information about what changes are expected. Other early questions may be more about the "self," with educators asking, "What is in it for me?" and "Why do I need to change?" Later, questions will be more focused on the activities required and how they can be fit into their many other duties. Later in the change process, individuals may focus more on impact and be concerned if the changes they are trying in their practice are working, how others are doing things differently, and if there is more to learn by sharing with others who are also working toward becoming critically cultural competent. Keeping the lines of communication open and acknowledging the concerns and questions educators have are very important tasks when trying to make changes or promote an innovation, such as moving toward developing critical cultural competence. As a resource for those planning which activities in this book will be most useful with different groups at different times during professional development about critical cultural competence, we offer Figure 8.3 Stages of Concern—The Concerns-Based Adoption Model (CBAM), which further describes CBAM as originally developed by Hord et al. (1987), generic expressions of concern that might be heard at each level, and specific questions or concerns that might be heard about critical cultural competence.

Additionally, in Resource 8.1 *Activities, Goals, and CBAM Levels for Developing Critical Cultural Competence*, located in the companion website for this book, we also provide a list of all the activities described in this book and their stated goals. Furthermore, the numbers in the column labeled CBAM levels indicate where we think each activity could potentially be used, based on the facilitators' assessment and understanding of the needs and questions of the participants.

Figure 8.3   Stages of Concern—The Concerns-Based Adoption Model (CBAM)

Stages of Concern	Generic Expressions of Concern	Questions/Concerns About Critical Cultural Competence
Level 0— Bringing awareness	I don't know anything about it (i.e., critical cultural competence).	I am not aware of this new concept. I don't see a need to change my views about diversity.
Level 1— Gathering information	What is it? What is this all about?	What is critical cultural competence? How is it the same or different from being culturally competent or culturally responsive?
Level 2— Making it personal	How will it affect me?	How will developing critical cultural competence affect me as an educator? Will I become a different kind of educator?
Level 3— Managing it all	How am I going to become skillful at this? How am I going to be able to manage my time to do this?	How do I find the time to apply the ideas of critical cultural competence while teaching? It is taking me more time to differentiate my instruction.
Level 4— Realizing potential benefits and consequences	How is this impacting my learners? How can I refine my skills to have more impact?	Are my students doing better because of my efforts to develop critical cultural competence? What else can I do to be a culturally responsive educator?
Level 5— Collaborating with others	How are others doing with this? How can I connect with others doing the same things?	How can I share what I am learning about my students, and their families and community, with other educators— and learn from them as well?
Level 6 — Refocusing and reenergizing	I have some insights I would like to share with others. I have some additional questions I would like to explore.	I think other educators should know what I have learned. I have additional information and insights that is working for with diverse students.

Modified from Hord, S. M., Rutherford, W. L., Huling-Austin, L., & Hall, G. E. (1987). *Taking charge of change.* Alexandria, VA: Association of Supervision and Curriculum Development.

Planning for Professional Development

Depending on the context in which professional development will take place, the time available, and the number of participants, the format may vary greatly. To design sessions that challenge all the participants, facilitators need to be thoughtful in adapting the activities shared in this book, given all the factors mentioned in this chapter. However, it is always important that the professional development (1) aims to develop critical cultural competence beyond just awareness of and knowledge about diverse cultures; (2) involves active participation and some risk taking; (3) positions students, families, and communities as equal partners in learning; and (4) leads to sustainable efforts to transform school cultures to make them culturally responsive and equitable for all students. Furthermore, no matter how many sessions and how much time facilitators have, professional development around developing critical cultural competence must be designed based on the needs and the starting point of the school or the group, and it must value and maximize the integration of all participants' beliefs, backgrounds, and experiences. In the next section, we provide suggestions to help facilitators plan short-term and long-term professional development sessions.

Before We Start

As in teaching, professional development is always more successful and meaningful if we know what our participants' needs are and how to build on their prior knowledge and experiences. To establish logical goals and objectives for professional development, we need an idea of where we are in the beginning and where we want to be in the end. This type of assessment is usually referred to as "gap analysis" in the business world, and it has been used in educational administration as well. In addition to using CBAM to determine participants' concerns, gap analysis allows us to see where our strengths and resources are and how we can best use them to achieve a particular goal. For a school or PLC, for example, professional development would be needs-based, and typically, we would start with "where we want to be" and then explore "where we are" so we can identify what our specific goals and objectives for professional development should be.

For example, in a school where a relatively large group of Vietnamese students have recently enrolled, educators may see a need for learning more about how to better serve their Vietnamese students and their families, and they may have specific goals they would like to achieve related to self, students, families, and communities. Resource 8.1 *Activities, Goals, and CBAM Levels for Developing Critical Cultural Competence*, which is located in the companion website for this book, lists some sample goals educators may focus on. The next step is to examine "where we are." Even though educators may not have had any experience working with Vietnamese students in their classrooms, they may have other relevant experiences and applicable resources. Educators' prior experiences working with other culturally and linguistically diverse groups or their familiarity with the local neighborhood and communities, for example, might be assets that we can build on throughout our professional development. After identifying where we want to be and where we are, our objectives for the professional development sessions can then be identified. Resource 8.2 *Sample Framework for Gap Analysis* is also located in the companion website for this book. This example can be used as a model for how to develop a gap analysis.

If you are leading professional development sessions at your school or in your district, you might have the advantage of already knowing what the schools and educators would like to achieve through the professional development sessions. If you are not as familiar with the educators you are working with, it might be a good idea to do an informal gap analysis with administrators or lead teachers to make your design for the proposed professional development more targeted toward the needs of the school or the group you will be working with. Here are some sample questions that could be used to explore where we want to be and where we are.

Where We Want to Be

- How was this need for professional development initiated? Why is it necessary?
- What does the school/district want to achieve through the professional development?
- What would be the ideal outcome for the professional development?

Where We Are

- What school/district professional development or programs have already been completed?
- How has the school/district successfully integrated new ideas or approaches in the past?
- What are some resources our educators, students, or community partners bring to address this topic?

Session Planning and Delivery

Any number of the activities listed in Resource 8.1, located in the companion website for this book, can be combined for professional development sessions of various lengths. Based on our sample gap analysis, Resource 8.3 contains a *Sample Two-Hour Professional Development Session Plan.*

Resource 8.4 contains a *Sample Plan for a Professional Learning Community (PLC)* with suggested activities that a PLC could undertake over a sustained period, perhaps a semester.

Resource 8.5 is an additional *Sample Professional Development Series Plan* for long-term professional development over the course of, perhaps, a school year. All three of these sample professional development plans are located in the companion website for this book. For the yearlong professional development, we also recommend using Resource 8.6 *Pre- and Postsurvey of Development of Critical Cultural Competence* to monitor participants' growth, which is also on the companion website for this book.

Pre- and Postassessment

As facilitators plan for a professional development series or for just a few sessions, we strongly encourage the use of pre- and postassessment (see Resource 8.6 Pre- and Postsurvey of Development of Critical Cultural Competence in the companion website for this book) to track the participants' development toward critical cultural competence. The preassessment could be used as an introduction to the concept of critical cultural competence. In addition to the session goals, concrete items on the preassessment could be used as an anticipation guide to prepare educators for the content of the professional development. Similarly, the postassessment could be used as a review of the content allowing participants to reflect on major content discussed or projects completed through the session. Further, if used as a self-assessment, the comparison of the pre- and postassessment allows participants to map their growth toward critical cultural competence, which could enhance their self-efficacy and metacognitive awareness to sustain development in the end. Finally, for facilitators, both pre- and postassessment data can provide essential feedback to guide further improvement for future professional development on similar topics.

The assessment plan we have provided can be conducted in different formats depending on the time limits and settings. Generally speaking, the facilitator may consider using Likert-scale items, open-ended questions, or a mixture of the two. Whichever format the facilitator decides to use, we recommend considering the participants' development of critical cultural competence from various perspectives that may include knowledge (cognitive), motivation (affective), skills (behavioral), and reflections (metacognitive). Building on the definition of critical cultural competence in the Preface, for example, Resource 8.6 *Pre- and Postsurvey of Development of Critical Cultural Competence* is just one sample pre- and postassessment that facilitators may consider adapting for their professional development sessions. Resource 4.5 also contains additional resources for survey instruments that can be used as is or modified, and it is also located on the companion website for this book.

The following blueprint correlates with Resource 8.6 *Pre- and Postsurvey of Development of Critical Cultural Competence*, and it is provided here to help facilitators select corresponding Likert-scale items that focus on different aspects of educators' critical cultural awareness development. The open-ended questions may have a focus on different aspects depending on educators' responses.

	Knowledge (cognitive)	Motivation (affective)	Skills (behavioral)	Reflections (metacognitive)
Self	1	2	3	4
Students	5	6	7	8
Families and communities	9	10	11	12

Follow-Up

To ensure the sustainable impact of professional development sessions, it is important that facilitators intentionally integrate ways to follow up with the participants after the actual sessions are over. It is always desirable for participants to leave professional development sessions with both new ideas and knowledge and also with actions to take. The action does not need to be very complex; however, it does need to be concrete and specific.

For example, one educator's action after the professional development session regarding working with Vietnamese students and their families might be "I will locate one website that provides good information regarding Vietnamese culture and summarize five tips for my peers by the end of next week." It is concrete that the educator knows exactly how to start (looking for websites), involves a product to be shared (summarizing five tips), and indicates a specific time (by the end of next week). Getting such commitments from educators at the end of professional development sessions could effectively extend the impact of the sessions and allow educators to generate new energy for further self-development.

E-mail communication is probably one of the easiest ways to follow up with participants. Typically, the facilitator collects e-mail addresses from the participants during the initial session and creates an e-mail list to follow up with participants immediately after the session, several weeks after, and then several months after. Sending follow-up e-mails is a great way for the facilitator to obtain session feedback from the participants and get ideas for the design of future professional development sessions. It could also serve as a reminder to encourage participants to apply and share the ideas they obtained from the professional development. Depending on availability and access, other communication tools, such as message boards, wikis, or blogs also could be used for the facilitator to follow up with participants or to initiate and facilitate follow-up collaborative projects among educators.

SUMMARY OF KEY POINTS

In this chapter, we linked the development of critical cultural competence to culturally responsive teaching, and we described how the tenets of both constructs are important for helping educators be culturally competent in their professional practice. We made the point that although safe activities may be a good place to begin the journey toward critical cultural competence, educators will have to get outside of the comfort of their classrooms and schools and into the communities to take the risk to learn about their students directly from their families and communities. We also discussed the important role that critical self-reflection plays in moving toward becoming more critically culturally competent and the need for professional development facilitators to provide appropriate feedback during discussions and debriefings to create the sense of "positive restlessness" (Kuh, 2007) that leads to change. We also recommended using Rogers's (2003) adoption of innovation theory and Hall and Hord's (1987) concerns-based adoption model (CBAM) as frameworks for helping to plan and differentiate professional develop for developing critical cultural competence, given that not all educators are at the same place in their understanding of or readiness for changing their practices to be more culturally responsive.

Before providing several plans for using the activities in this book for short-term and long-term professional development, we suggested doing a gap analysis and also collaborating with others leaders. Several ways to assess the success of such professional development are also discussed, as is our final suggestion about following up with participants in your professional development sessions.

FINAL WORDS

Throughout this book, we provided numerous concrete, interactive, and challenging activities that be used in professional development settings to move educators beyond just knowledge about the cultural diversity of today's students. Our goal is to encourage all educators to move forward on the path to *critical* cultural competence so they can better understand themselves as cultural beings and develop the habit of critical reflection that leads to transformative action in education. We believe this can be accomplished best by learning from and with families and communities to develop a deeper, more nuanced understanding of how to reach and challenge all students to achieve their potential. Therefore, our approach to professional development for critical cultural competence positions students, families, and communities as equal partners with educators by engaging them in mutual learning and teaching experiences. Through active participation in intentional experiences with guided reflection, we hope educators will have the opportunity to take risks and explore ways to become the learners of their students and their families within and beyond classroom settings (Delpit, 1995; Gay, 2010). The outcome of such professional development can lead to sustainable efforts in schools to reform and transform school cultures so education is accessible and equitable for all.

ADDITIONAL RESOURCES

In Resource 8.7 *Authors' Favorite Readings and Resources*, located on the companion website for this book, we provide a list or books and other resources that we recommend to anyone engaged in developing critical cultural competence. These readings have influenced and extended our thinking about the self, students, families, and communities. We hope you use these to further educate yourself and others.

REFLECTION AND EXTENSION

- Where and with whom will you lead your next professional development session?
- What is the first step you want to take to plan for your facilitation?
- How would you know that you successfully challenged educators' critical cultural competence development?

ONLINE EXTENSIONS

- For more information about CBAM, including online surveys and reporting tools available to show where your educators regarding their levels of concern over the course of professional development, SEDL, formerly the Southeast Educational Development Laboratory in Austin, TX, is a great resource. Go to www.sedl.org/cbam/.

- SEDL also provides excellent information about PLCs at www
  .sedl.org/change/issues/issues61/outcomes.html.
- Additional assessments could also be found at www.sit.edu/
  SITOccasionalPapers/feil_appendix_f.pdf.

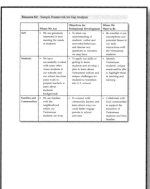

References

Applebaum, B. (2003). White privilege, complicity, and the social construction of race. *Educational Foundations, 17*(4), 5–20

Arias, M. B., & Morillo-Campbell, M. (2008). *Promoting ELL parental involvement: Challenges in contested times.* The Great Lakes Center for Education Research & Practice. Retrieved from http://www.greatlakescenter.org/docs/Policy_Briefs?Arias_ELL.pdf

Banks, C. A. M., & Banks, J. A. (1995). Equity pedagogy: An essential component of multicultural education. *Theory into Practice, 34*(3), 152–158.

Banks, J. A. (2001). Citizenship education and diversity: Implications for teacher education. *Journal of Teacher Education, 52*(1), 5–16.

Banks, J. A. (2006). *Cultural diversity and education: Foundations, curriculum and teaching* (5th ed.). Boston, MA: Pearson Education.

Boyle-Baise, M. (2005). Preparing community-oriented teachers: Reflections from a multicultural service-learning project. *Journal of Teacher Education, 56,* 446–458.

Boyle-Baise, M., & Sleeter, C. E. (1998). *Community service learning for multicultural teacher education.* Washington, DC: Education Resources Information Center. Retrieved from ERIC database. (ED429925)

Brown-Jeffy, S., & Cooper, J. E. (2011). Toward a conceptual framework of culturally relevant pedagogy: An overview of the conceptual and theoretical literature. *Teacher Education Quarterly, 38*(1), 65–84.

Buehl, M. M., & Fives, H. (2009). Exploring teachers' beliefs about teaching knowledge: Where does it come from? Does it change? *The Journal of Experimental Education, 77*(4), 367–407.

Burant, T. J., & Kirby, D. (2002). Beyond classroom-based early field experiences: Understanding an "educative practicum" in an urban school and community. *Teaching and Teacher Education, 18,* 561–575.

Capps, R., Fix, M., Murray, J., Ost, J., Passel, J., & Herwantoro-Hernandez, S. (2005). *The new demography of America's schools: Immigration and the No Child Left Behind Act.* Washington, DC: Urban Institute.

Carter, M., Cadge, W., Rivero, E., & Curran, S. (2002). Designing your community-based learning project: Five questions to ask about your pedagogical and participatory goals. *Teaching Sociology, 30*(2), 158–173.

Chant, R. H. (2009). Developing involved and active citizens: The role of personal practical theories and action research in a standards-based social studies classroom. *Teacher Education Quarterly, 36*(4), 181–90.

Chant, R. H., Heafner, T. L., & Bennett, K. R. (2004). Connecting personal theorizing and action research to preservice teacher development. *Teacher Education Quarterly, 31*(3), 25–42.

Clair, N., & Adger, C. T. (1999). *Professional development for teachers in culturally diverse schools.* ERIC Clearinghouse on Languages and Linguistics. Retrieved from http://www.cal.org/resources/digest/digest_pdfs/9908-clair-profdvpt.pdf

Cochran-Smith, M., & Fries, M. K. (2001). Sticks, stones, and ideology: The discourse of reform in teacher education. *Educational Researcher, 30*(3), 3–14.

Cooper, J. E. (2007). Strengthening the case for community-based learning in teacher education. *Journal of Teacher Education, 58*(3), 245–255.

Council for Exceptional Children. (n.d.). *CEC performance-based standards.* Retrieved from http://www.cec.sped.org/ps/perf_based_stds/standards.html

Cramer, K. D., & Wasiak, H. (2006). *Change the way you see everything: Through asset-based thinking.* Philadelphia, PA: Running Press.

Cross T., Bazron, B., Dennis, K., & Isaacs, M. (1989). *Towards a culturally competent system of care,* (Vol. 1). Washington, DC: Georgetown University Child Development Center, CASSP Technical Assistance Center.

Daniels, H. (2002). *Literature circles: Voice and choice in book clubs and reading groups.* Portsmouth, NH: Heinemann.

Darling-Hammond, L., & Bransford, J. (Eds.). (2005). *Preparing teachers for a changing world: What teachers should learn and be able to do.* San Francisco: Jossey-Bass.

Dee, J. R., & Henkin, A. B. (2002). Assessing dispositions toward cultural diversity among preservice teachers. *Urban Education, 37*(1), 22–40.

Delandshere, G., & Petrosky, A. (2004). Political rationales and ideological stances of the standards-based reform of teacher education in the US. *Teaching and Teacher Education, 20*(1), 1–15.

Delpit, L. (1995). *Other people's children: Cultural conflict in the classroom.* New York, NY: The New Press.

Delpit, L. (2010). The silenced dialogue: Power and pedagogy in educating other people's children. In E. F. Provenzo, Jr. (Ed.), *The teacher in American society* (pp. 97–120). Thousand Oaks, CA: Sage.

Department of Education. (2010). *Supporting families and communities: Reauthorizing the Elementary and Secondary Education Act.* Retrieved from http://www2.ed.gov/policy/elsec/leg/blueprint/faq/supporting-family.pdf

Duffy, G. G. (2002). Visioning and the development of outstanding teachers. *Reading Research and Instruction, 41,* 331–344.

Duffy, G. G., & Hoffman, J. V. (1999). In pursuit of an illusion: The flawed search for a perfect method. *Reading Teacher, 53*(1), 10–17.

El-Haj, T. R. (2003). Practicing for equity from the standpoint of the particular: Exploring the work of one urban teacher network. *Teachers College Record, 105,* 817–845.

Epstein, J. L. (1995). School/family/community partnerships: Caring for the children we share. *Phi Delta Kappan, 76,* 701–712.

Epstein, J. (2001). *School, family, and community partnerships: Preparing educators and improving schools.* Boulder, CO: Westview Press.

Epstein, J. L., & Sanders, M. G. (2006). Prospects for change: Preparing educators for school, family, and community partnerships. *Peabody Journal of Education, 81*(2), 81–120.

Estrada, P. (2005). The courage to grow: A researcher and teacher linking professional development with small-group reading instruction and student achievement. *Research in the Teaching of English, 39*(4), 320–364.

Fairbanks, C. M., Duffy, G. G., Faircloth, B. S., He, Y. Levin, B. B., Rohr, J., & Stein, C. (2010). Beyond knowledge: Exploring why some teachers are more thoughtfully adaptive than others. *Journal of Teacher Education, 61*(1/2), 161–171.

Fenton, M. (Ed.). (2006, November). *The PTA News: The Official Letter of the Parent-Teacher Association of PS261.* Retrieved from http://www.ps261.org/news/archive/200611.pdf

Fickel, E. H. (2005). Teachers, tundra, and talking circles: Learning history and culture in an Alaskan native village. *Theory and Research in Social Education, 33*(4), 476–507.

Finkbeiner, C., & Koplin, C. (2002). *A cooperative approach for facilitating intercultural education.* Reading Online. Retrieved from http//www.reading online.org/newliteracies/lit_index.asp?HREF=finkbeiner/index.html

Fives, H., & Buehl, M. M. (2008). What do teachers believe? Developing a framework for examining beliefs about teachers' knowledge and ability. *Contemporary Educational Psychology, 33*(2), 134–176.

Fuller-Thomson, E., & Minkler, M. (2001). American grandparents providing extensive childcare to their grandchildren: Prevalence and profile. *The Gerontologist, 41,* 201–209.

Gajda, R. (2004). Responding to the needs of the adopted child. *Kappa Delta Pi Record, 40*(4), 160–164.

Gay, G. (2002). Preparing for culturally responsive teaching. *Journal of Teacher Education, 53*(2), 106–116.

Gay, G. (2010). Acting on beliefs in teacher education for cultural diversity. *Journal of Teacher Education, 61*(1/2), 143–152.

Gelnaw, A., Brickley, M., Marsh, H., & Ryan, D. (2004). *Opening doors: Lesbian and gay parents and schools.* Washington, DC: Family Pride Coalition.

Genzuk, M. (1999). Tapping into community funds of knowledge. In *Effective strategies for English language acquisition: Curriculum guide for professional development of teachers grades kindergarten through eight* (pp. 9–21). Los Angeles, CA: Los Angeles Annenberg Metropolitan Project.

Gilmore, D. P., & Bell, K. (2006). We are family: Using diverse family structure literature with children. *Reading Horizons, 46,* 279–299.

Gollnick, D. M., & Chinn, P. C. (2004). *Multicultural education in a pluralistic society* (6th ed.). New York, NY: Prentice Hall.

Gonzalez, N., Moll, L., & Amanti, C. (2005). *Funds of knowledge: Theorizing practices in households, communities, and classrooms.* Mahwah, NJ: Lawrence Erlbaum.

Goodenough, W. (1963). *Cooperation in change: An anthropological approach to community development.* New York, NY: Russell Sage Foundation.

Gordon, M. F., & Louis, K. S. (2009). Linking parent and community involvement with student achievement: Comparing principal and teacher perceptions of stakeholder influence. *American Journal of Education, 116*(1), 1–31.

Grant, C., Elsbree, A. R., & Fondrie, S. (2004). A decade of research on the changing terrain of multicultural education research. In J. A. Banks & C. A. M. Banks (Eds.), *Handbook of research on multicultural education* (2nd ed., pp. 184–207). San Francisco, CA: Jossey-Bass.

Grant, C., & Sleeter, C. (2006). *Turning on learning: Five approaches to multicultural teaching plans for race, class, gender, and disability* (4th ed.). Upper Saddle River, NJ: Prentice-Hall.

Grant, K. B., & Ray, J. A. (2010). *Home, school, and community collaboration: Culturally responsive family involvement.* Thousand Oaks, CA: Sage.

Hall, G. E., & Hord, S. M. (1987). *Change in schools: Facilitating the process.* Albany: State University of New York Press.

Hammerness, K. (2003). Learning to hope, or hoping to learn? The role of vision in the early professional lives of teachers. *Journal of Teacher Education, 54*(1), 43–56.

Hammerness, K. (2006). *Seeing through teachers' eyes: Professional ideals and classroom practices.* New York, NY: Teachers College Press.

Hammerness, K., Darling-Hammond, L., & Bransford, J. (with Berliner, D., Cochran-Smith, M., McDonald, M., & Zeichner, K.). (2005). How teachers learn and develop. In L. Darling-Hammond & J. Bransford (Eds.), *Preparing teachers for a changing world* (pp 358–389). San Francisco, CA: Jossey-Bass.

Harvey, S., & Goudvis, A. (2007). *Strategies that work: Teaching comprehension for understanding and engagement* (2nd ed.). Portsmouth, NH: Heinemann.

Hatton, N., & Smith, D. (1995). Reflection in teacher education: Towards definition and implementation. *Teaching and Teacher Education, 11*(1), 33–49.

Hawes, C. A., & Plourde, L. A. (2005). Parental involvement and its influence on the reading achievement of 6th grade students. *Reading Improvement, 42*(1), 47–57.

He, Y., & Cooper, J. E. (2009). The ABCs for preservice teacher cultural competency development. *Teaching Education, 20*(3), 305–322.

He, Y., & Levin, B. (2008). Match or mismatch? How congruent are the beliefs of teacher candidates, teacher educators, and field mentors? *Teacher Education Quarterly, 35*(4), 37–55.

Henderson, A., & Mapp, K. (2002). *A new wave of evidence: The impact of school, family, and community connections on student achievement.* Austin, TX: National Center for Family and Community Connections with Schools.

Herrera, S. (2010). *Biography-driven culturally responsive teaching.* New York, NY: Teachers College Press.

Hill, N. E., & Craft, S. A. (2003). Parent–school involvement and school performance: Mediated pathways among socioeconomically comparable African American and Euro-American families. *Journal of Educational Psychology, 95*(1), 74–83.

Hobbs, N. (1978). Classification options: A conversation with Nicholas Hobbs on exceptional child education. *Exceptional Children, 44*, 494–497.

Hong, S., & Ho, H. (2005). Direct and indirect longitudinal effects of parental involvement on student achievement: Second-order latent growth modeling across ethnic groups. *Journal of Educational Psychology, 97*(1), 32–42.

Hord, S. M. (1997). *Professional learning communities: Communities of continuous inquiry and improvement.* Austin, TX: Southwest Educational Development Laboratory.

Hord, S. M., Rutherford, W. L., Huling-Austin, L., & Hall, G. E. (1987). *Taking charge of change.* Alexandria, VA: Association of Supervision and Curriculum Development.

Howard, G. R. (2006). *We can't teach what we don't know: White teachers, multiracial schools.* (2nd ed.). New York, NY: Teacher College Press.

Hubbard, R. S., & Power, B. M. (2003). *The art of classroom inquiry: A handbook for teacher researchers.* Portsmouth, NH: Heinemann.

Interstate New Teacher Assessment and Support Consortium. (1992). *Model core teaching standards: A resource for state dialogue.* Retrieved from http://cehhs.utk.edu/ncate/utir/cf/cf.6.pdf

Ivey, A. E., & Ivey, M. B. (2007). *Intentional interviewing and counseling: Facilitating client development in a multicultural society.* Pacific Grove, CA: Brooks/Cole-Thompson Learning.

James, E. (2009). *Children of divorce: The shocking statistics.* Retrieved from http://www.articlesbase.com/divorce-articles/children-of-divorce-the-shocking-statistics-833765.html

Jenks, C., Lee, J. O., & Kanpol, B. (2001). Approaches to multicultural education in preservice teacher education: Philosophical frameworks and models for teaching. *Urban Review, 33*(2), 87–105.

Jennings, L. B., & Smith, C. P. (2002). Examining the role of critical inquiry for transformative practices. *Teachers College Record, 104*(3), 456–481.

Jewett, S. (2006). If you don't identify with your ancestry, you're like a race without a land: Constructing race at a small urban middle school. *Anthropology and Education Quarterly, 37*(1), 144–161.

Jeynes, W. H. (2007). The relationship between parental involvement and urban secondary school student academic achievement: A meta-analysis. *Urban Education, 42*(1), 82–110.

Jezewski, M. A., & Sotnik, P. (2001). *The rehabilitation service provider as culture broker: Providing culturally competent services to foreign born persons.* Buffalo, NY: Center for International Rehabilitation Research Information and Exchange.

Johns, B. H., Crowley, E. P., & Guetzloe, E. (2001). *Effective curriculum for students with emotional and behavioral disorders: Reaching them through teaching them.* Denver, CO: Love.

Jost, A., Whitfield, E. L., & Jost, M. (2005). When the rules are fair but the game isn't. *Multicultural Education, 13*(1), 14–21.

Kemmis, S., & McTaggart, R. (Eds.). (1988). *The action research planner* (3rd. ed.). Geelong, Victoria: Deakin University Press.

Kennedy, M. (2006). Knowledge and vision in teaching. *Journal of Teacher Education, 57*(3), 205–211.

Khanna, N., & Harris, C. A. (2009). Teaching race as a social construction: Two interactive class exercises. *Teaching Sociology, 37*, 369–378.

Kozleski, B., Pugach, M., & Yinger, R. (2002, February). *Preparing teachers to work with students with disabilities: Possibilities and challenges for special and general teacher education: A white paper.* Washington, DC: American Association of Colleges for Teacher Education. Retrieved from ERIC database. (ED468743)

Kuh, G. D. (2007). Success in college. In P. Lingenfelter (Ed.), *More student success: A systemic solution,* pp. 95–107. Boulder, CO: State Higher Education Executive Officers.

Kurtts, S. A., Ponder, G., & Cooper, J. E. (2006). Integrating systems of care philosophy and practices into schools: The perspectives of special education and general education. In C. Herrick & M. Arbuckle (Eds.), *Interdisciplinary Practice: Systems of Care.* (pp. 267–289). Sudbury, MA: Jones & Bartlett.

Ladson-Billings, G. (1995). But that's just good teaching! The case for culturally relevant pedagogy. *Theory into Practice, 34*(3), 159–165.

Ladson-Billings, G. (2001). *Crossing over to Canaan: The journey of new teachers in diverse classrooms.* San Francisco, CA: Jossey-Bass.

Lee, J. (2002). Racial and ethnic achievement gap trends: Reversing the progress toward equity? *Educational Researcher, 31*(3), 3–12.

Leistyna, P. (2001). Extending the possibilities of multicultural professional development in public schools. *Journal of Curriculum and Supervision, 16*(4), 282–304.

Levin, B. B., & He, Y. (2008). Investigating the content and sources of preservice teachers' personal practical theories (PPTs). *Journal of Teacher Education,* 59(1), 55–68.

Levin, B. B., & He, Y., & Allen, M. A. (2010, April). *What do they believe now? A cross-sectional longitudinal follow-up study of teachers' beliefs in action.* Paper presented at the annual meeting of the American Educational Research Association, Denver, CO.

Lott, B. (2001). Low-income parents and the public schools. *Journal of Social Issues, 57,* 247–259.

Lustig, M. W., & Koester, J. (2003). *Intercultural competence: Interpersonal communication across cultures.* Boston, MA: Allyn and Bacon.

Lytle, S., & Cochran-Smith, M. (1990). Learning from teacher research: A working typology. *Teachers College Record, 92*(1), 83–103.

McDiarmid, G. W. (1992). What to do about differences? A study of multicultural education for teacher trainees in the Los Angeles Unified School District. *Journal of Teacher Education, 43*(2), 83–93.

McIntosh, P. (1990). White privilege: Unpacking the invisible knapsack. *Independent School, 49*(2), 31–36.

McLaren, P. (2006). *Life in schools: An introduction to critical pedagogy in the foundations of education* (5th ed.). Boston, MA: Allyn & Bacon.

McNaughton, D., & Vostal, B. (2010). Using active listening to improve collaboration with parents: The LAFF don't CRY strategy. *Intervention in School and Clinic, 45,* 251–256.

Milner, H. R. IV. (2010). What does teacher education have to do with teaching? Implications for diversity studies. *Journal of Teacher Education, 61,* 118–131.

Moll, L. C., & González, N. (1994). Lessons from research with language-minority children. *Journal of Reading Behavior, 26*(4), 439–456.

Moll, L. C., & Greenberg, J. M. (1990). Creating zones of possibilities: Combining social constructs for instruction. In L. C. Moll (Ed.), *Vygotsky and education: Instructional implications and applications of sociohistorical psychology.* (pp. 319–348). New York, NY: Cambridge Press.

Mooney, L. A., & Edwards, B. (2001). Experiential learning in sociology: Service learning and other community-based learning initiatives. *Teaching Sociology, 29*(2), 181–194.

Moss, G. (2001). Critical pedagogy: Translation for education that is multicultural. *Multicultural Education, 9*(2), 2–11.

Murrell, P. C. (2001). *The community teacher: A new framework for effective urban teaching.* New York, NY: Teachers College Press.

National Board of Professional Teaching Standards. (n.d.). *What teachers should know and be able to do.* Retrieved from http://www.nbpts.org/pdf/coreprops.pdf

National Council for the Accreditation of Teacher Education. (n.d.). *NCATE unit standards.* Retrieved from http://www.ncate.org/public/standards.asp

Nieto, S. (2000). Placing equity front and center: Some thoughts on transforming teacher education in a new century. *Journal of Teacher Education, 51*(3), 180–187.

Nieto, S. (2003). Challenging current notions of "highly qualified teachers" through work in a teachers' inquiry group. *Journal of Teacher Education, 54*(5), 386–398.

Nieto, S., & Bode, P. (2008). *Affirming diversity: The sociopolitical context of multicultural education* (5th ed.). Boston, MA: Allyn & Bacon.

Oberg, A., & McCutcheon, G. (1987). Teachers' experience doing action research. *Peabody Journal of Education, 64*(2), 116–128.

Officialmoviepage.com. (2010). The official movie site of Mad Hot Ballroom (2005). Retrieved from http://officialmoviepage.com/mad-hot-ballroom.

Owens, T. R., & Wang, C. (1996). *Community-based learning: A foundation for meaningful educational reform* (Northwest Regional Education Laboratory, School Improvement Research Series). Retrieved from http://www.nwrel.org/scpd/sirs/10/t008.html

Paek, P. L. (2008). *Practices worthy of attention: Local innovations in strengthening secondary mathematics.* Austin, TX: The Charles A. Dana Center at the University of Texas at Austin.

Pajares, M. F. (1992). Teacher's beliefs and educational research: Cleaning up a messy construct. *Review of Educational Research, 62*(3), 307–322.

Parent/Teacher Home Visit Project, The. (2011). *The parent/teacher home visit project.* Retrieved from http://www.pthvp.org/

Parents as Teachers. (n.d.). *Vision.* Retrieved from http://www.parentsasteachers.org/about/what-we-do/visionmission-history

Raphael, T. (1994). Collaboration on the book club project: The multiple roles of researchers, teachers, and students. *Reading Horizons, 34,* 381–405.

Rattigan-Rohr, J. P. (2005). *The examination of prospective teachers' initial and developing vision* (Doctoral dissertation). Available from Dissertations & Theses at University of North Carolina at Greensboro. (Publication No. AAT 3182835).

Richardson, V. (1996). The role of attitudes and beliefs in learning to teach. In J. Sikula (Ed.), *Handbook of research on teacher education* (2nd ed., pp. 102–119). New York, NY: Simon & Schuster.

Richardson, V. (2003). Preservice teachers' beliefs. In J. Raths & A. McAninch (Eds.). *Teacher beliefs and teacher education. Advances in teacher education* (pp. 1–22). Greenwich, CT: Information Age.

Rogers, E. M. (2003). *Diffusion of innovations* (5th ed.). New York, NY: Free Press.

Rong, X. L., & Preissle, J. (2009). *Educating immigrant students in the 21st century: What educators need to know.* Thousand Oaks, CA: Corwin.

Rothstein, R. (2004). A wider lens on the achievement gap. *Phi Delta Kappan, 86*(2), 104–110.

Saleebey, D. (1992). *The strengths perspective in social work practice.* White Plains, NY: Longman.

Schmidt, P. R. (1999). Know thyself and understand others. *Language Arts, 76,* 332–340.

Schmidt, P. R. (2001). The power to empower. In P. R. Schmidt & P. B. Mosenthal (Eds.). *Reconceptualizing literacy in the new age of multiculturalism and pluralism* (pp. 389–443). Greenwich, CT: Information Age.

Schmidt, P. R., & Finkbeiner, C. (2006). What is the ABCs of cultural understanding and communication? In P. R. Schmidt & C. Finkbeiner (Eds.), *The ABCs of cultural understanding and communication: National and international adaptations* (pp. 1–18). Greenwich, CT: Information Age.

Schön, D. A. (1983). *The reflective practitioner: How professionals think in action.* New York, NY: Basic Books.

Schön, D. A. (1996). *Educating the reflective practitioner: Toward a new design for teaching and learning in the professions.* San Francisco, CA: Jossey-Bass.

Shim, S., & Serido, J. (2010). *Wave 1.5 economic impact study: Financial well-being, coping behaviors and trust among young adults.* National Endowment for Financial Education (NEFE). Retrieved from http://aplus.arizona.edu/wave1_5_report.pdf

Shulman, L. (1987). Knowledge and teaching: Foundations of the new reform. *Harvard Educational Review, 57*(1), 1–22.

Shulman, L. (2004). Professional development: Leaning from experience. In S. Wilson (Ed.), *The wisdom of practice: Essays on teaching, learning, and learning to teach* (pp. 503–522). San Francisco, CA: Jossey-Bass.

Shulman, L., & Shulman, J. (2004). How and what teachers learn: A shifting perspective. *Journal of Curriculum Studies, 36,* 257–271.

Simon, B. S. (2001). Family involvement in high school: Predictors and effects. *NASSP Bulletin, 85*(2), 8–19.

Sleeter, C. E. (1992). *Keepers of the American dream.* London, UK: Falmer Press.

Sleeter, C. E. (2000). Strengthening multicultural education with community-based service learning. In C. R. O'Grady (Ed.), *Integrating service learning and multicultural education in colleges and universities* (pp. 263–276). Mahwah, NJ: Lawrence Erlbaum.

Sleeter, C. E. (2001). Preparing teachers for culturally diverse schools: Research and the overwhelming presence of whiteness. *Journal of Teacher Education, 52*(2), 94–106.

Sleeter, C. E. (2009). Developing teacher epistemological sophistication about multicultural curriculum: A case study. *Action in Teacher Education, 31*(1), 3–13.

Smith, J., & Wohlstetter, P. (2009). *Parent involvement in urban charter schools: A new paradigm or the status quo?* (Report prepared for School Choice and Improvement: Research in State, District and Community Contexts, Vanderbilt University). Retrieved from http://www.vanderbilt.edu/schoolchoice/conference/papers/Smith-Wohlstetter_COMPLETE.pdf

Smith, R. W. (2000). The influence of teacher background on the inclusion of multicultural education: A case study of two contrasts. *Urban Review, 32*(2), 155–176.

Snyder, C. R. (1995). Conceptualizing, measuring, and nurturing hope. *Journal of Counseling and Development, 73,* 355–360.

Supporting Families and Communities: Reauthorizing the Elementary and Secondary Education Act. (2010). Retrieved from http://www2.ed.gov/policy/elsec/leg/blueprint/faq/supporting-family.pdf

Teaching English to Speakers of Other Languages (TESOL). (2007). *TESOL standards for P–12 teacher education programs.* Retrieved from http://www.tesol.org/s_tesol/seccss.asp?CID=219&DID=1689

Thiagarajan, S. (2006). *Barnga: A simulation game on cultural clashes.* (3rd ed.). Boston, MA: Intercultural Press.

U.S. Census Bureau. (2005). *Population profile of the United States.* Retrieved from http://www.census.gov/population/www/pop-profile/files/dynamic/poverty.pdf

Vanneman, A., Hamilton, L., Anderson, J. B., & Rahman, T. (2009). *Achievement gaps: How Black and White students in public schools perform in mathematics and reading on the national assessment of educational progress.* Retrieved from http://nces.ed.gov/nationsreportcard/pdf/studies/2009455.pdf

Villegas, A. M., & Lucas, T. (2002). *Educating culturally responsive teachers: A coherent approach.* Albany: State University of New York Press.

Vygotsky, L. (1978). *Mind in society.* Cambridge, MA: Harvard University Press.

Wideen, M., Mayer-Smith, J., & Moon, B. (1998). A critical analysis of the research on learning to teach: Making the case for an ecological perspective on inquiry. *Review of Educational Research, 68*(2), 130–178.

Wiggins, G., & McTighe, J. (2005). *Understanding by design.* Alexandria, VA: Association for Supervision and Curriculum Development.

Zeichner, K. (1993). *Educating teachers for cultural diversity.* East Lansing, MI: National Center for Research on Teacher Learning, Michigan State University.

Zeichner, K. (2010). Rethinking the connections between campus courses and field experiences in college- and university-based teacher education. *Journal of Teacher Education, 61*(1), 89–99.

Zumwalt, K., & Craig, E. (2005). Teacher's characteristics: Research on the demographic profile. In Cochran-Smith, M., & Zeichner, K. (Eds.), *Studying teacher education: The report of the AERA Panel on Research and Teacher Education* (pp. 111–156). Mahwah, NJ: Lawrence Erlbaum.

Index

CORWIN

A SAGE Company

The Corwin logo—a raven striding across an open book—represents the union of courage and learning. Corwin is committed to improving education for all learners by publishing books and other professional development resources for those serving the field of PreK–12 education. By providing practical, hands-on materials, Corwin continues to carry out the promise of its motto: **"Helping Educators Do Their Work Better."**